Silicon Souls - Faces of the Future - Book 3

Journey Through the Faces of Tomorrow's Technology

Nixie Bytecraft

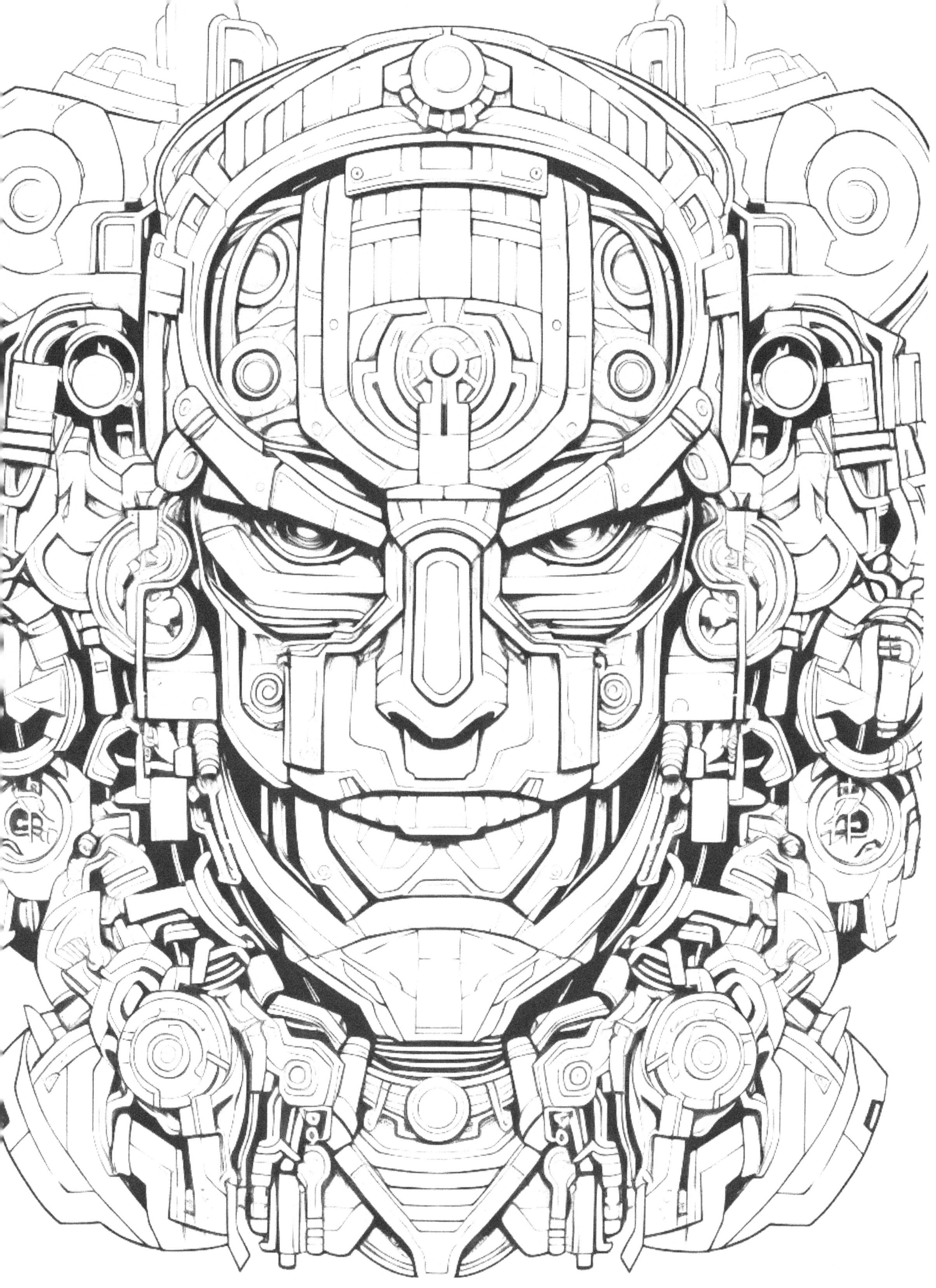

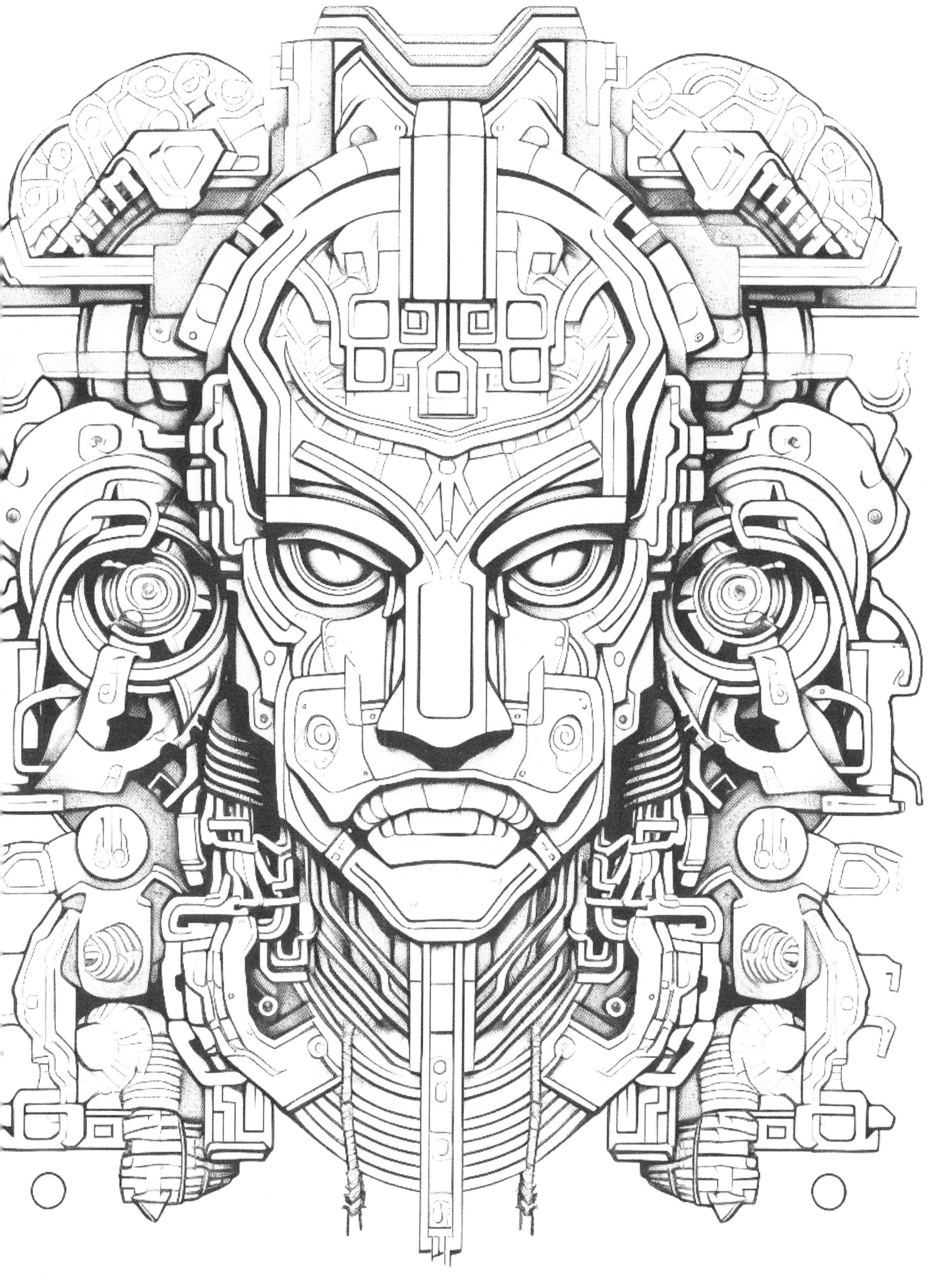

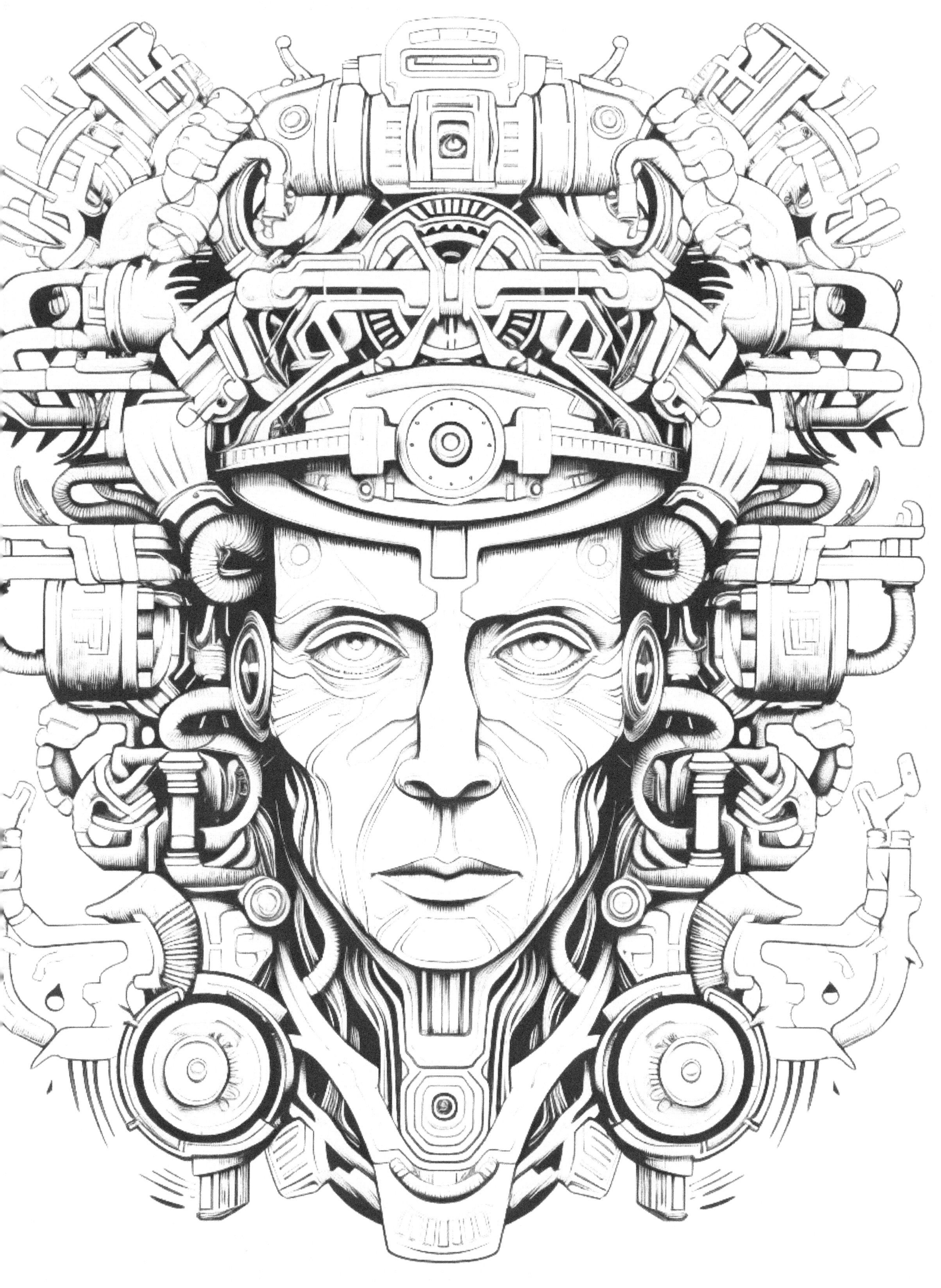

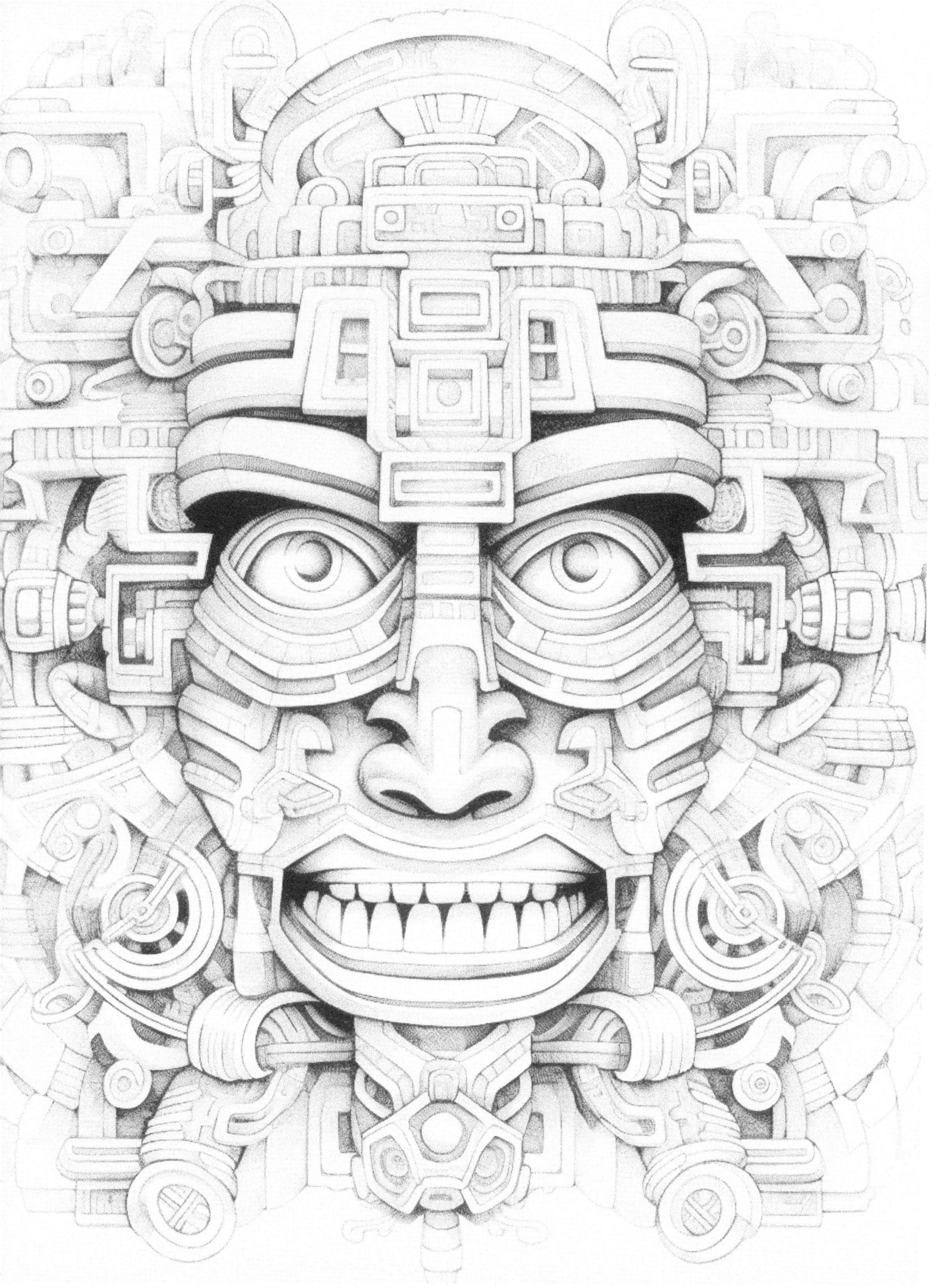

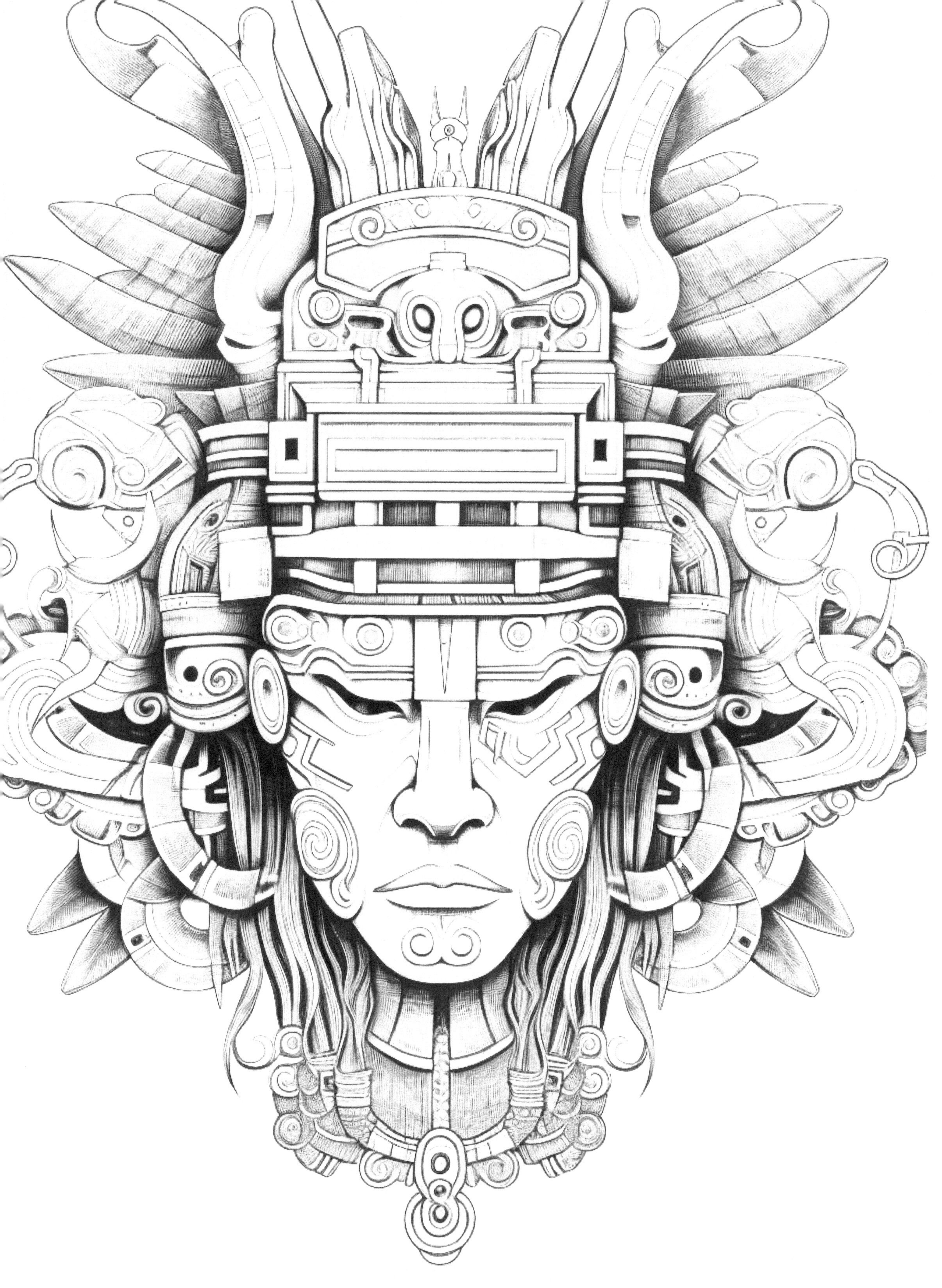

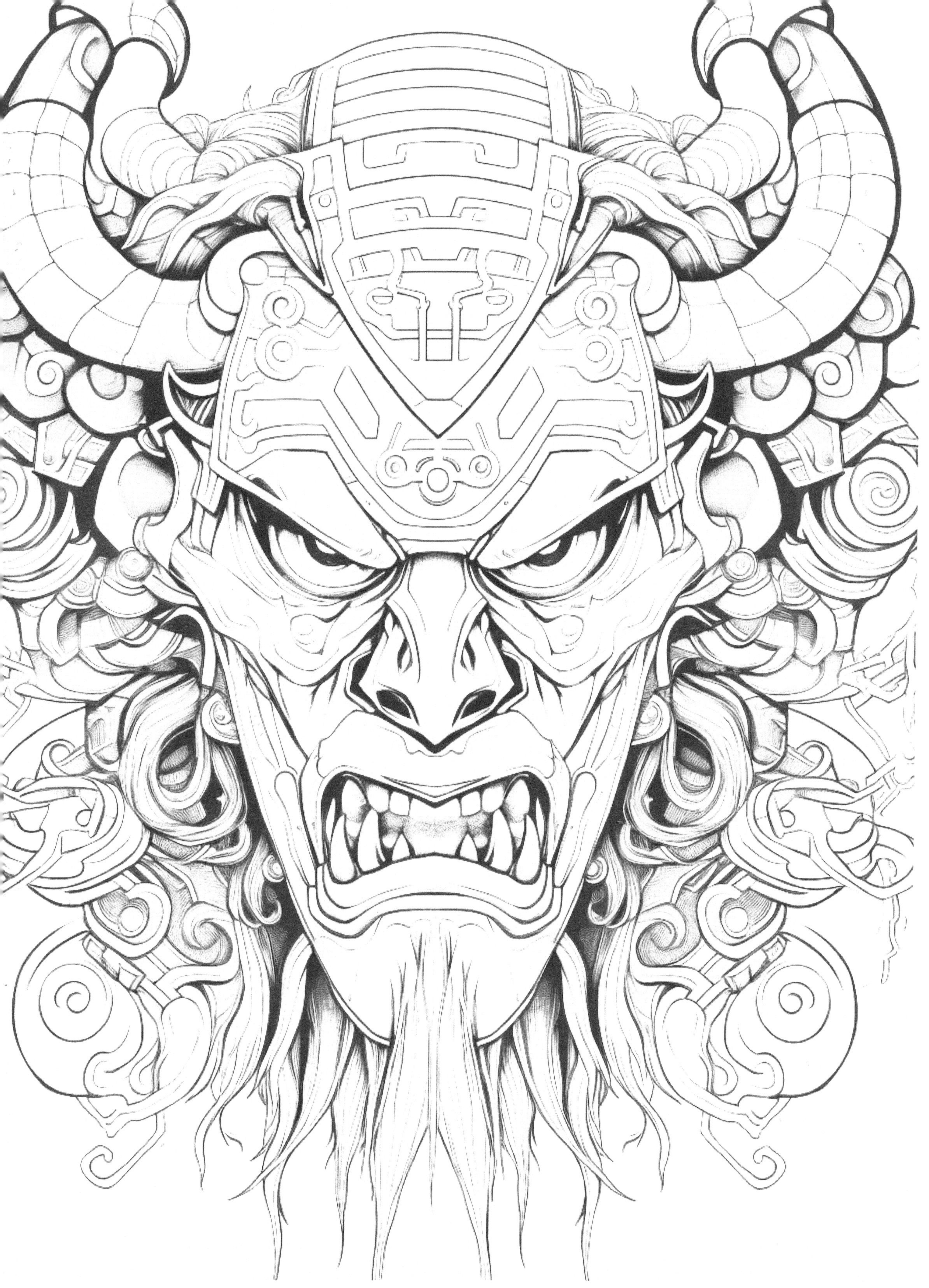

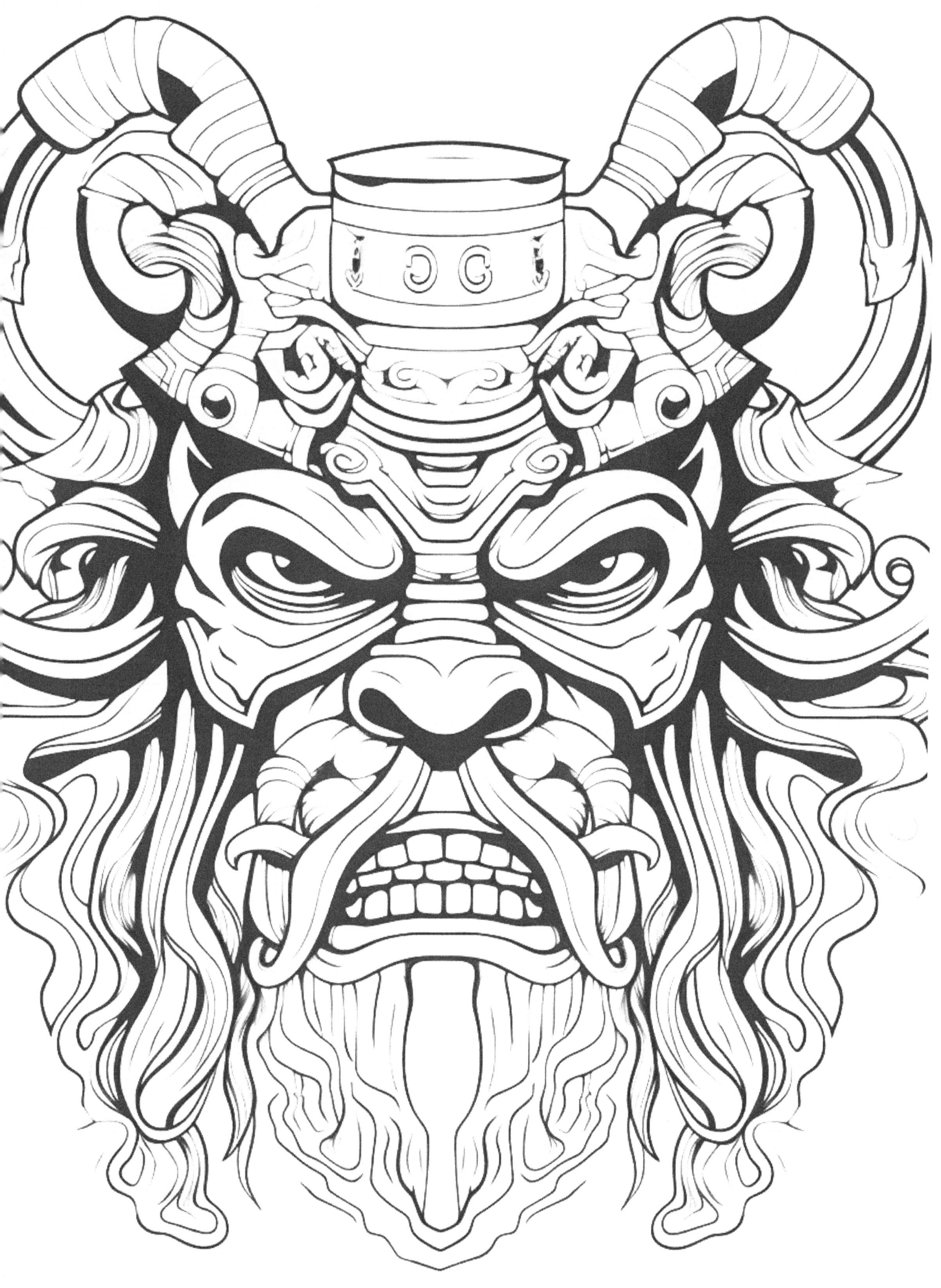

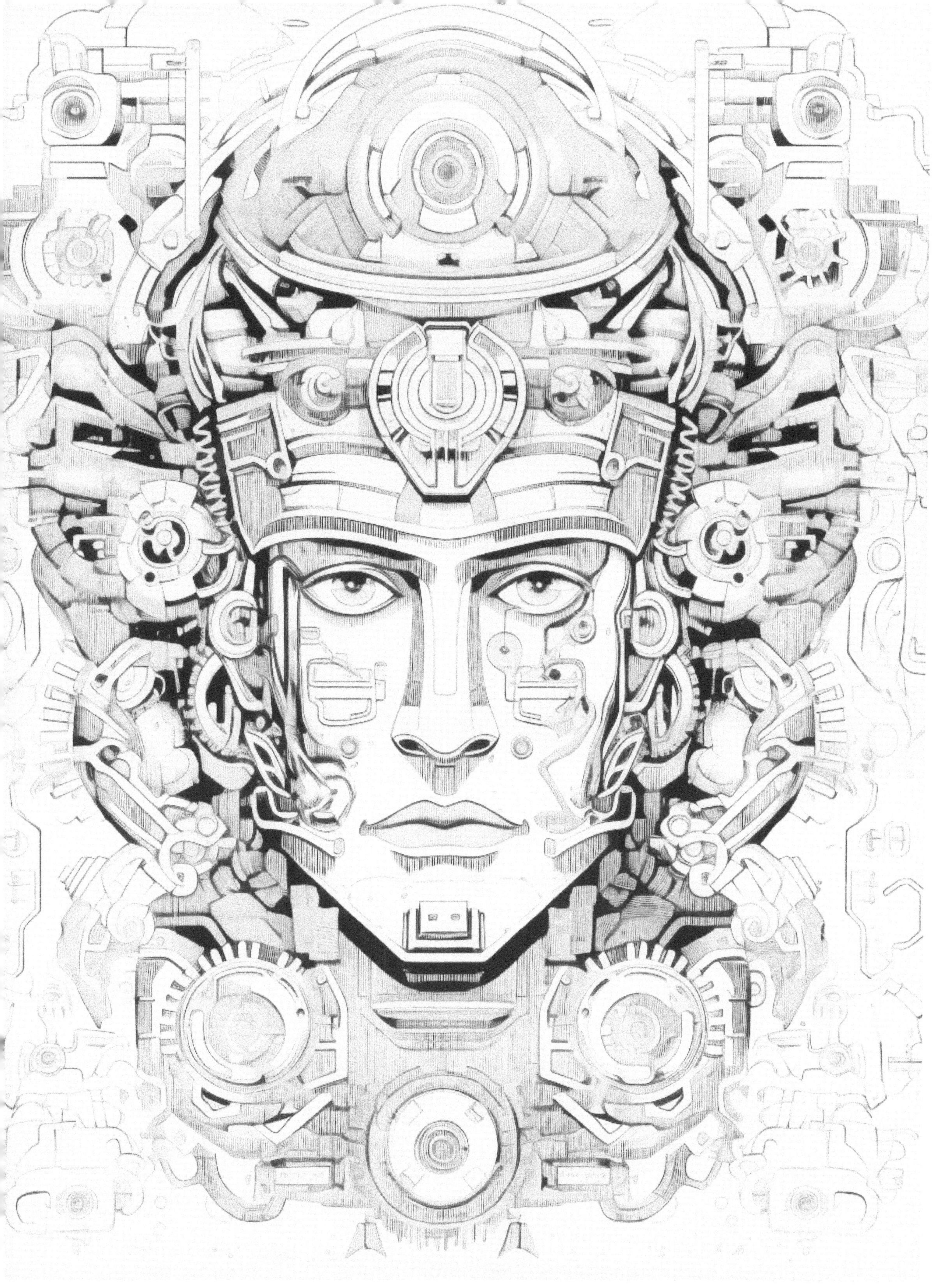

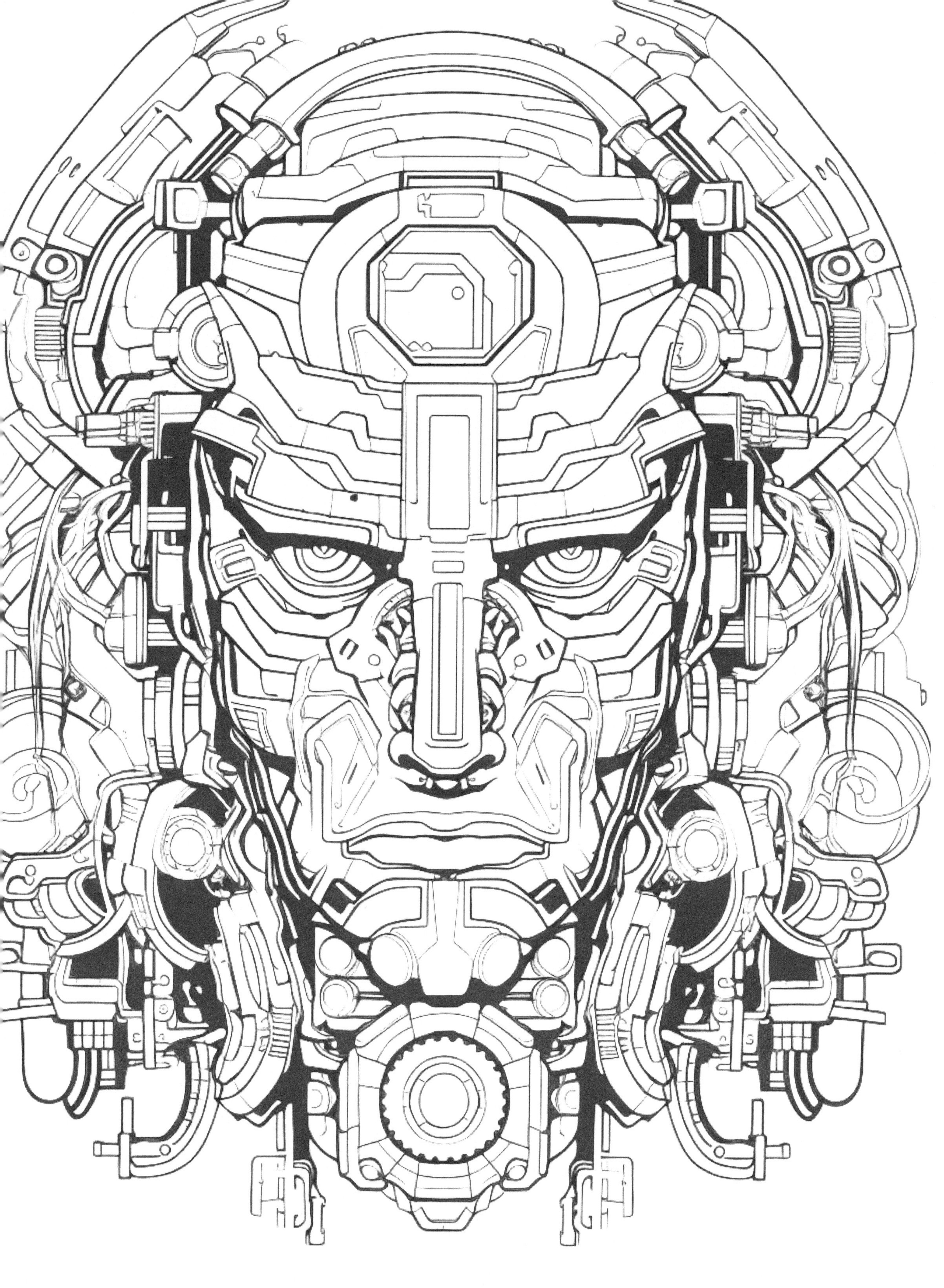

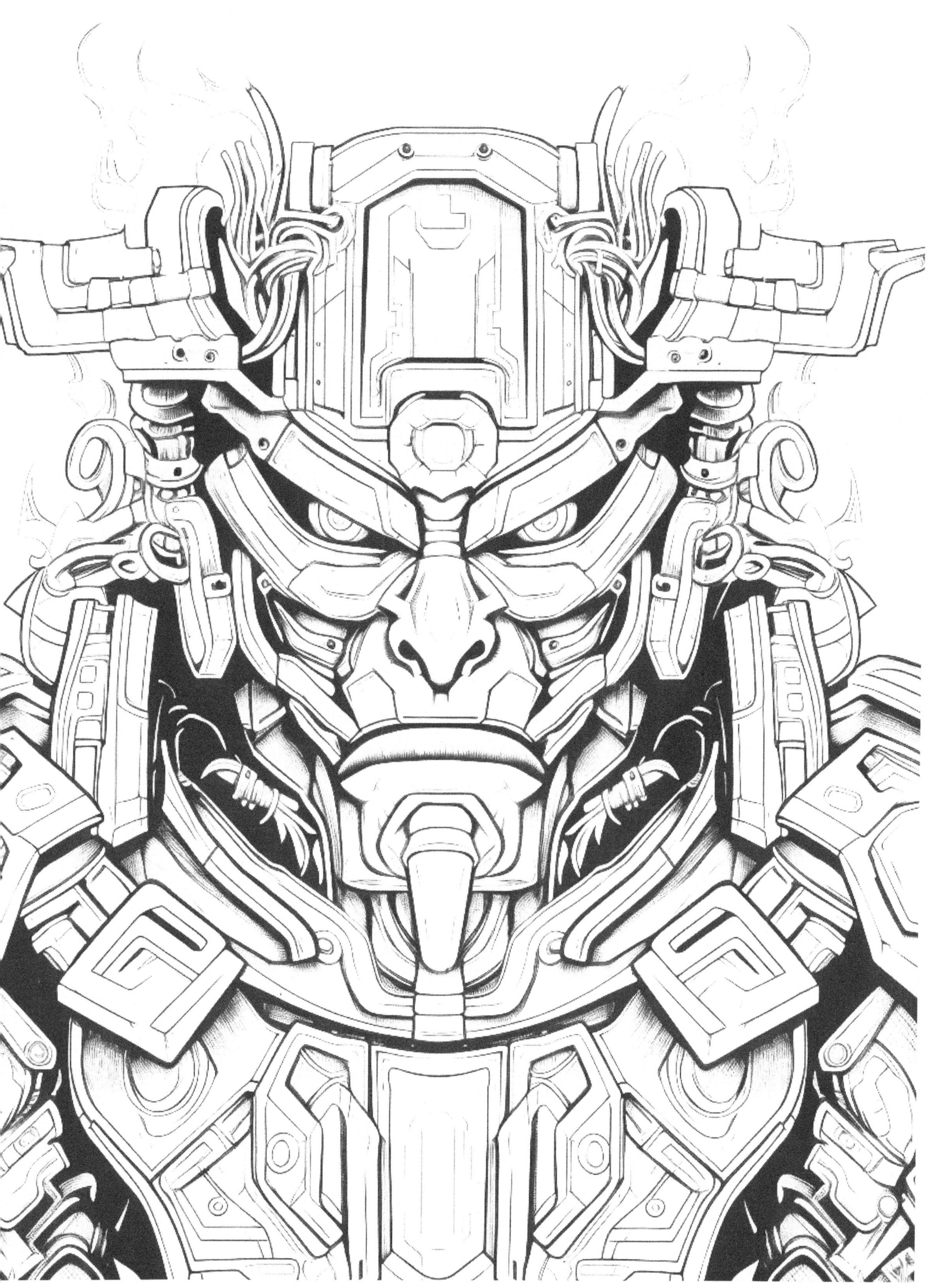

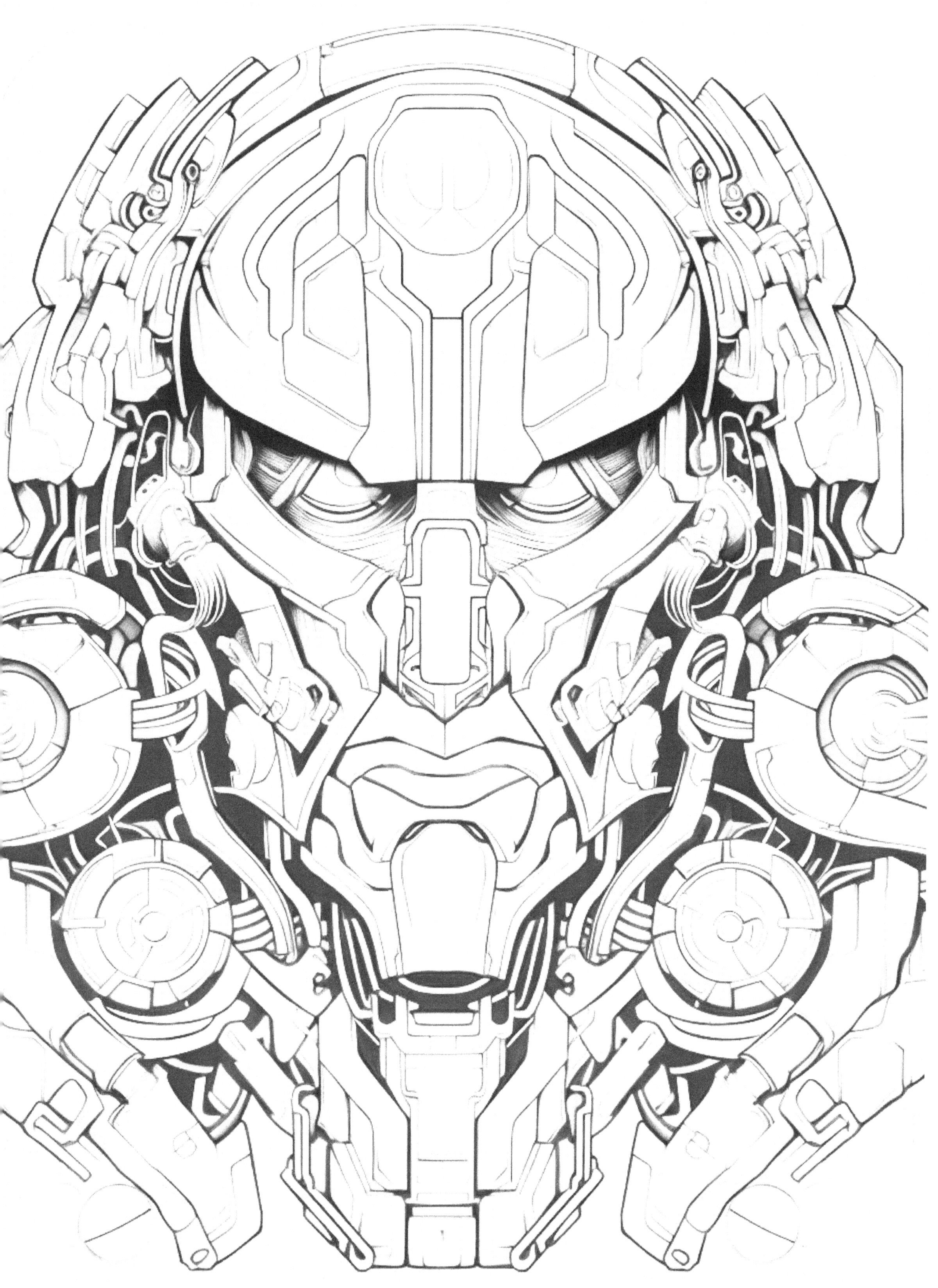

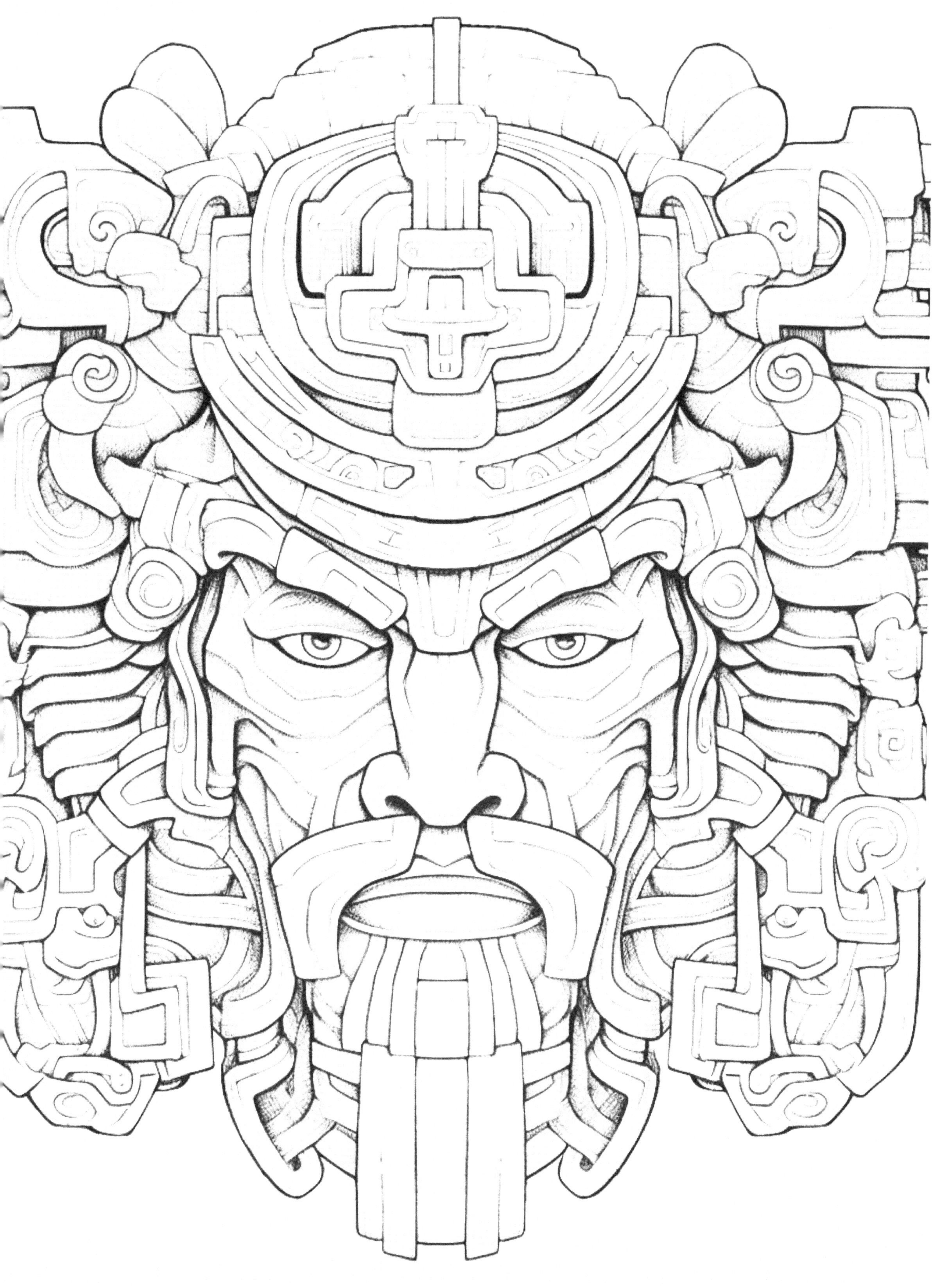

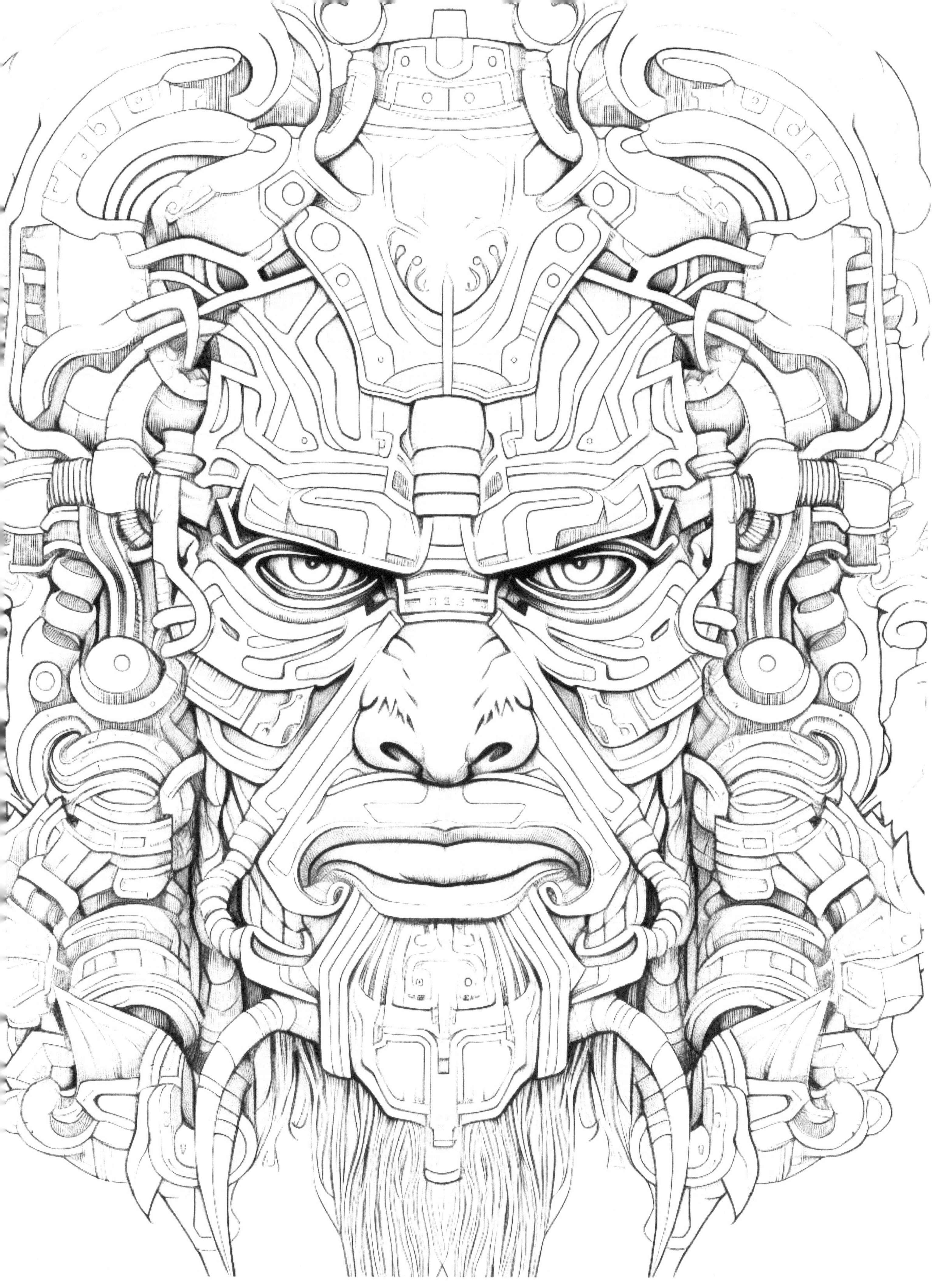

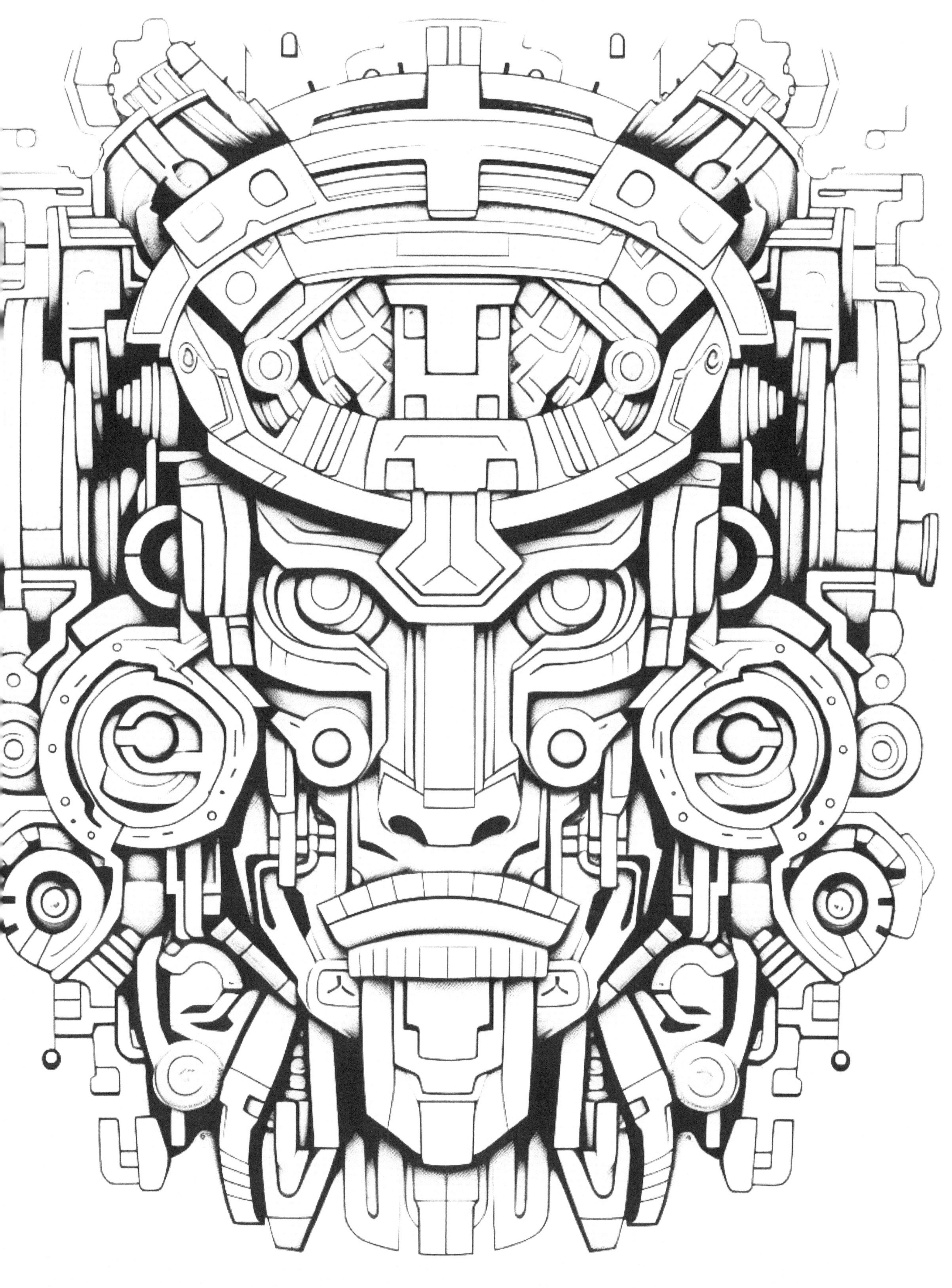

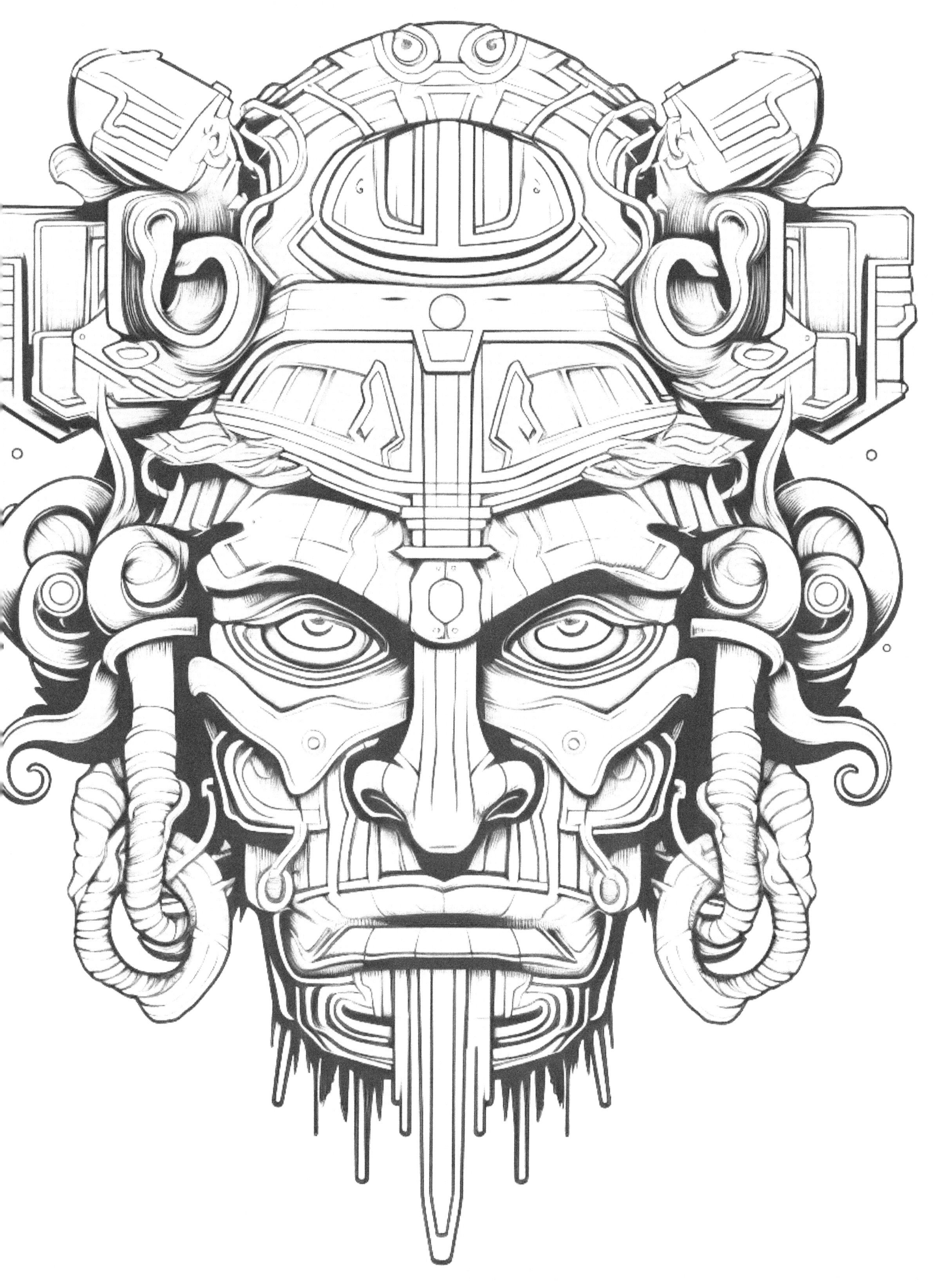

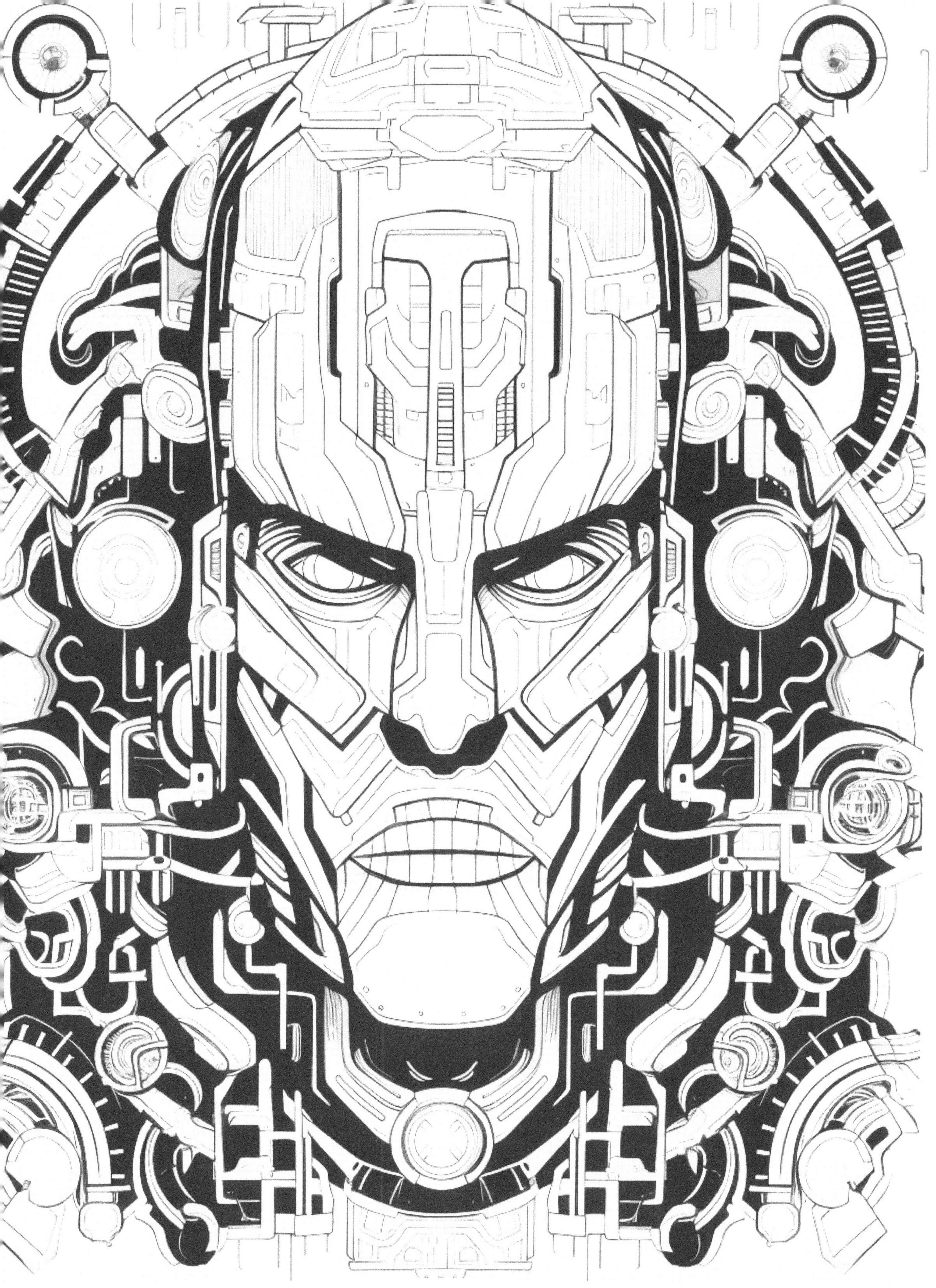

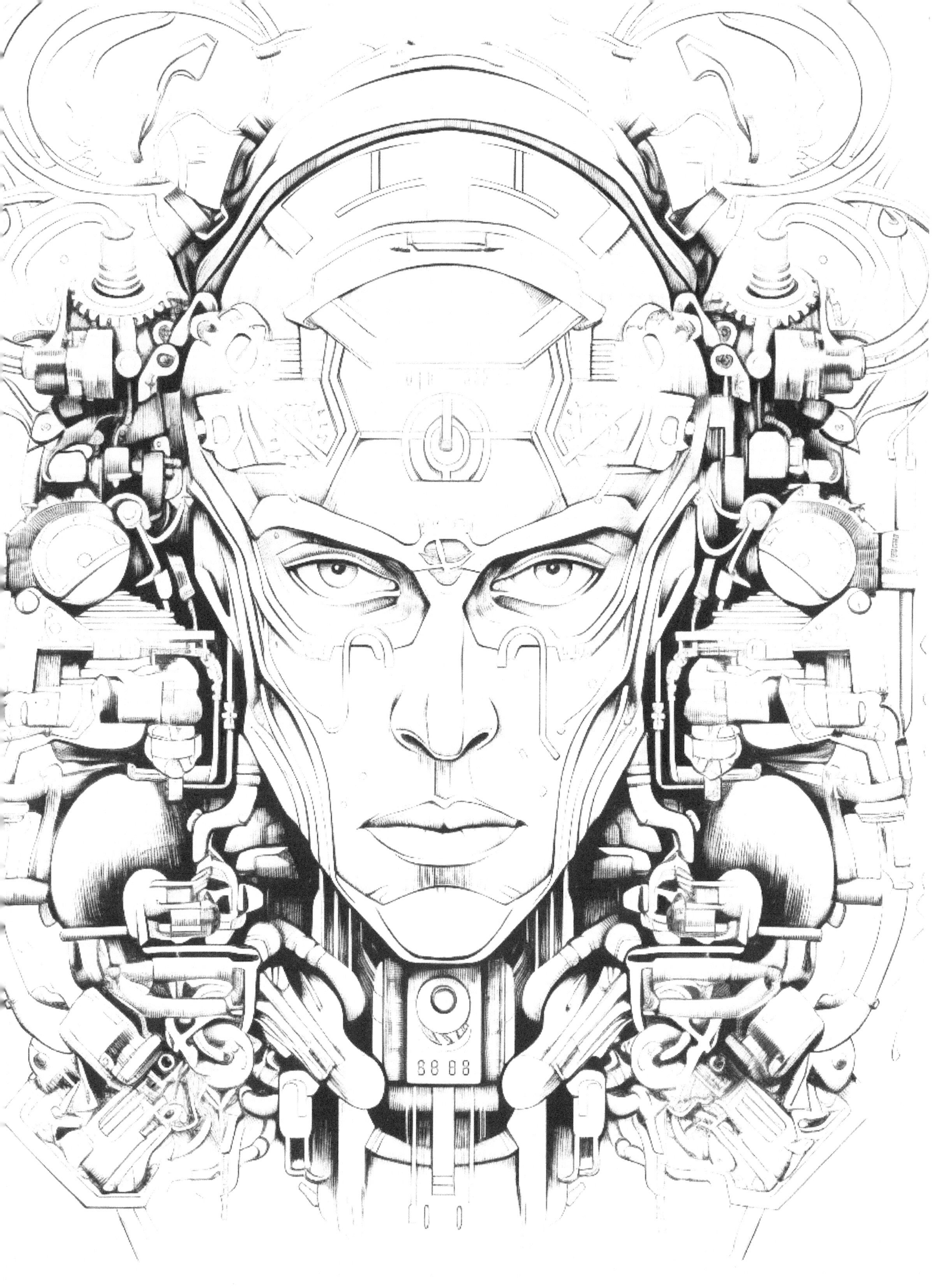

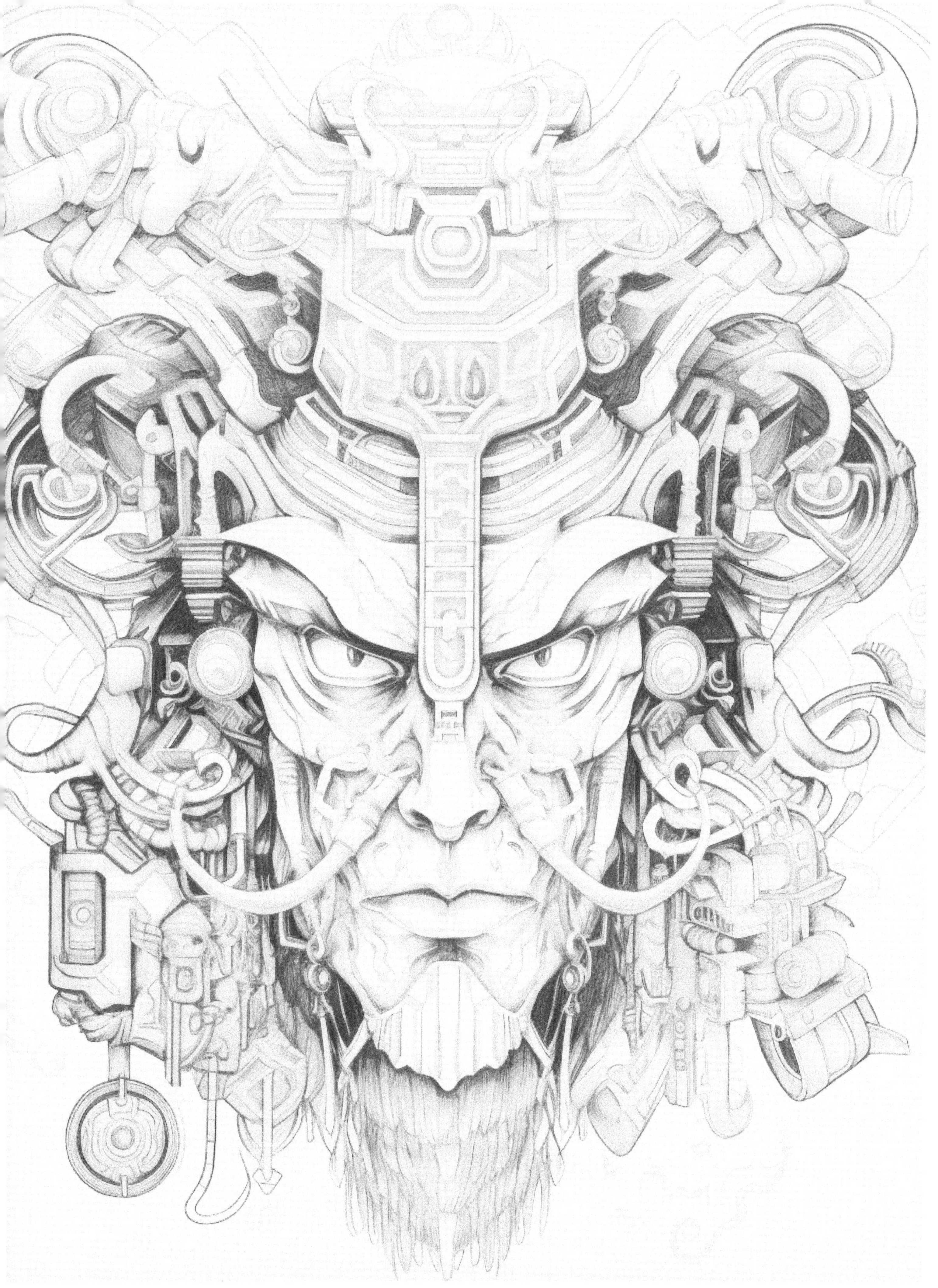

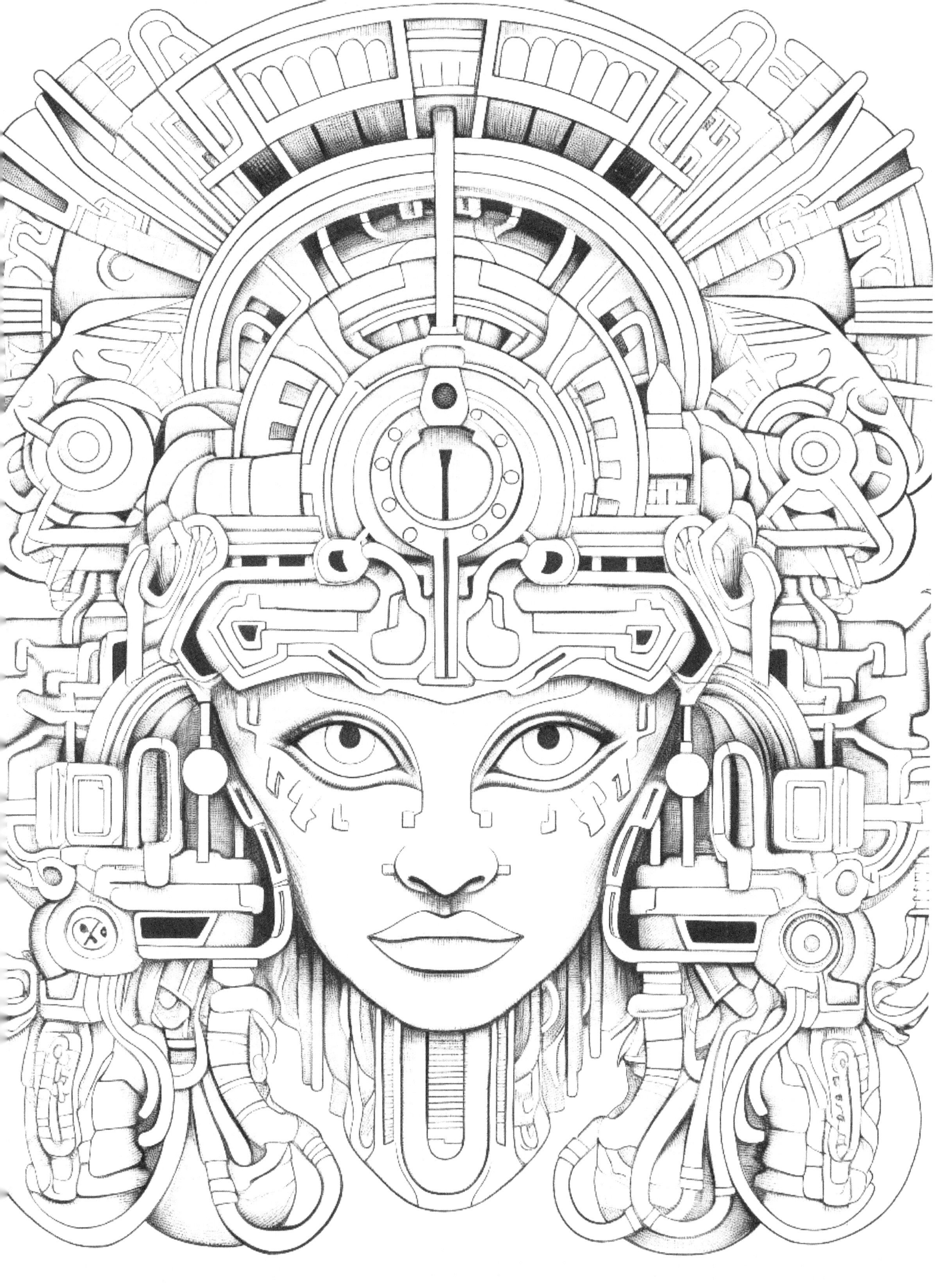

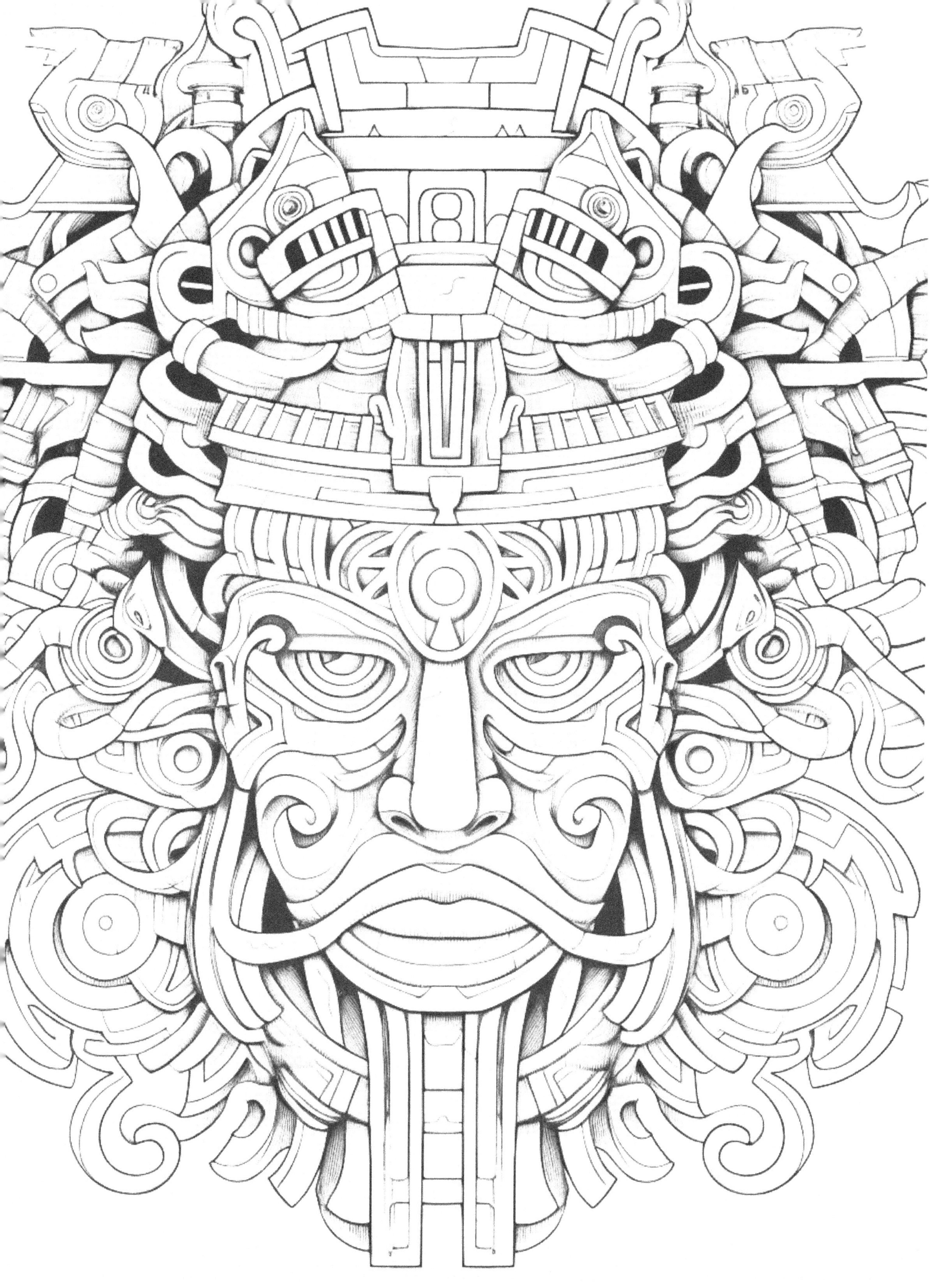

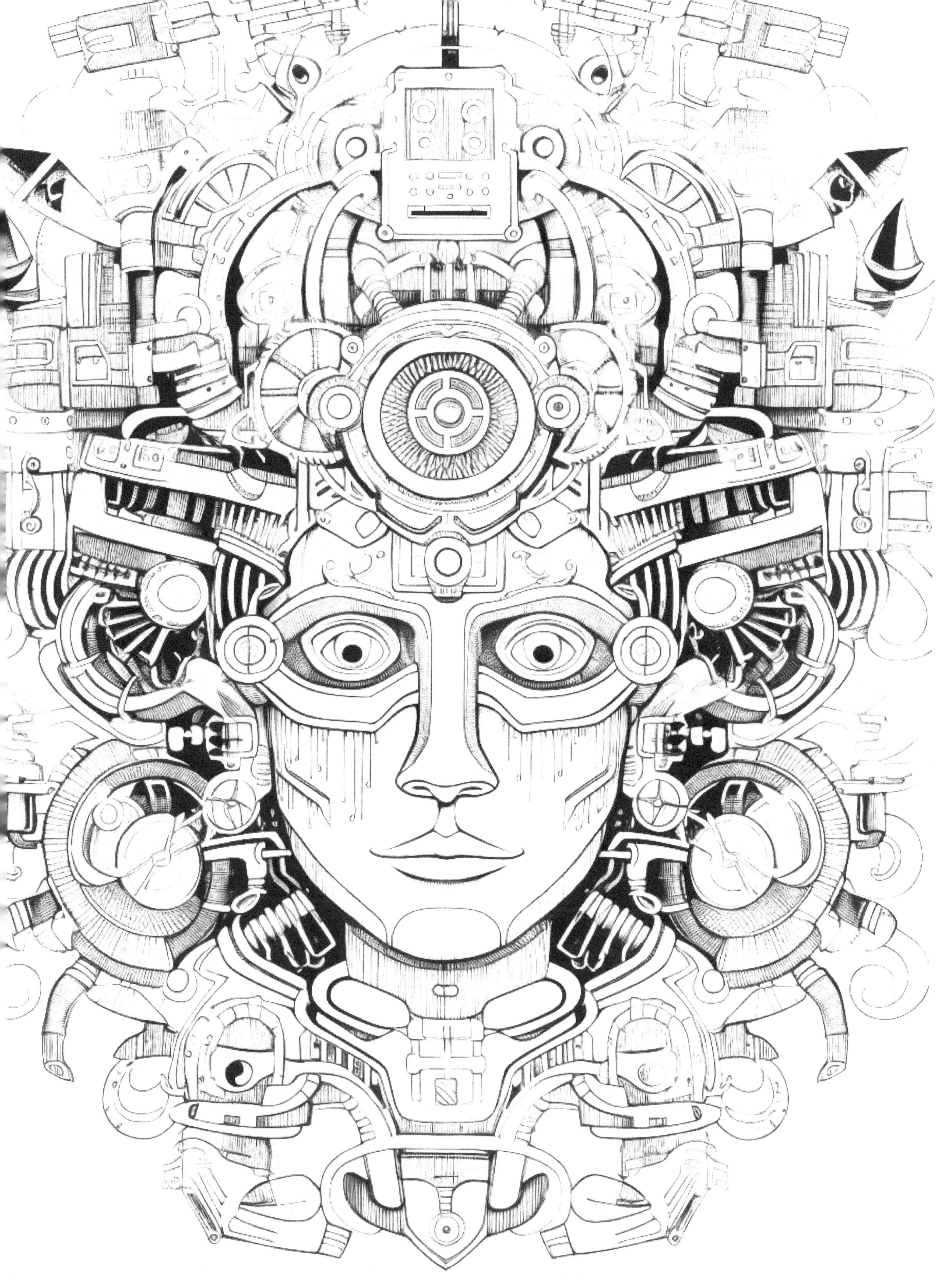

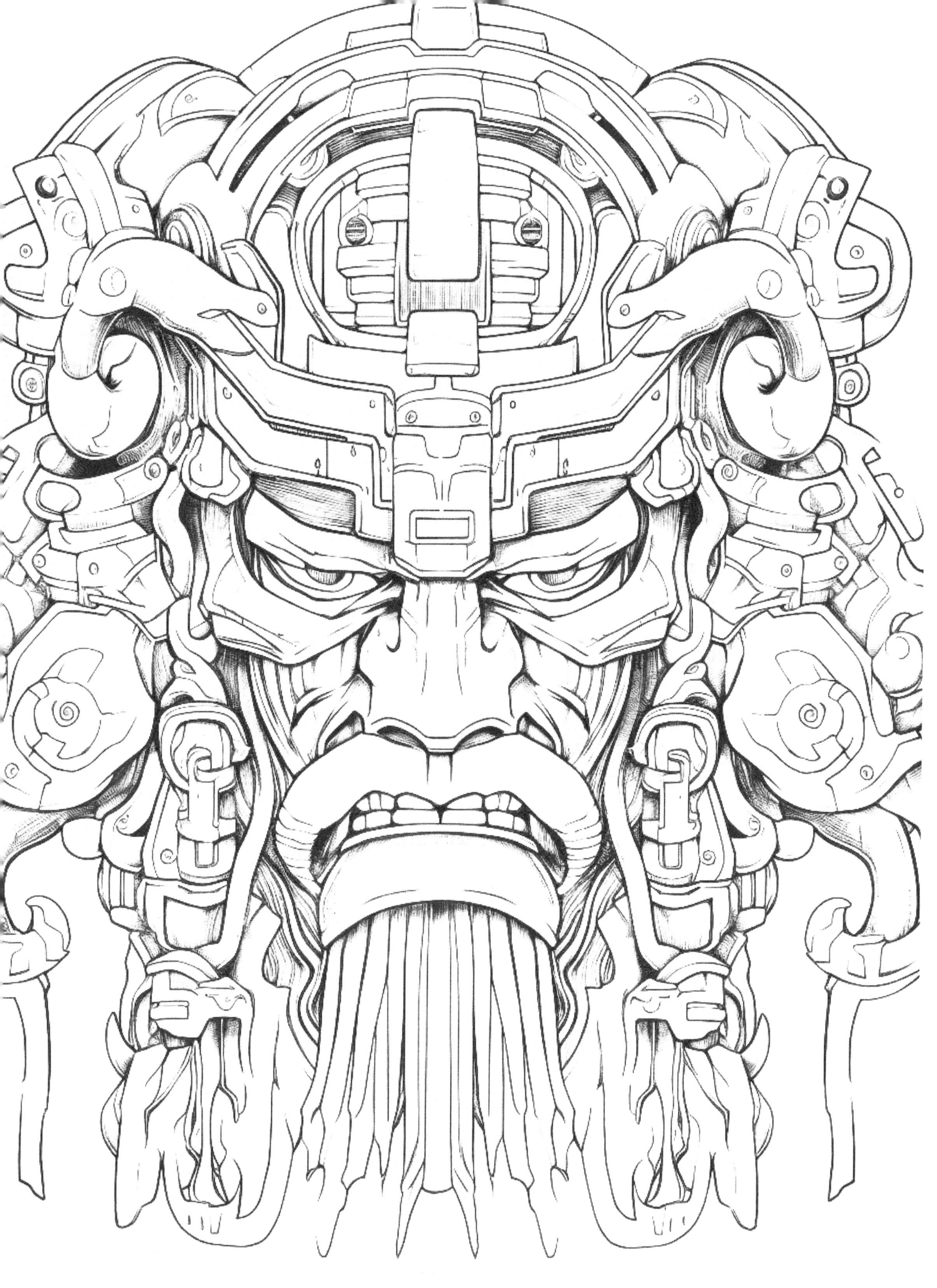

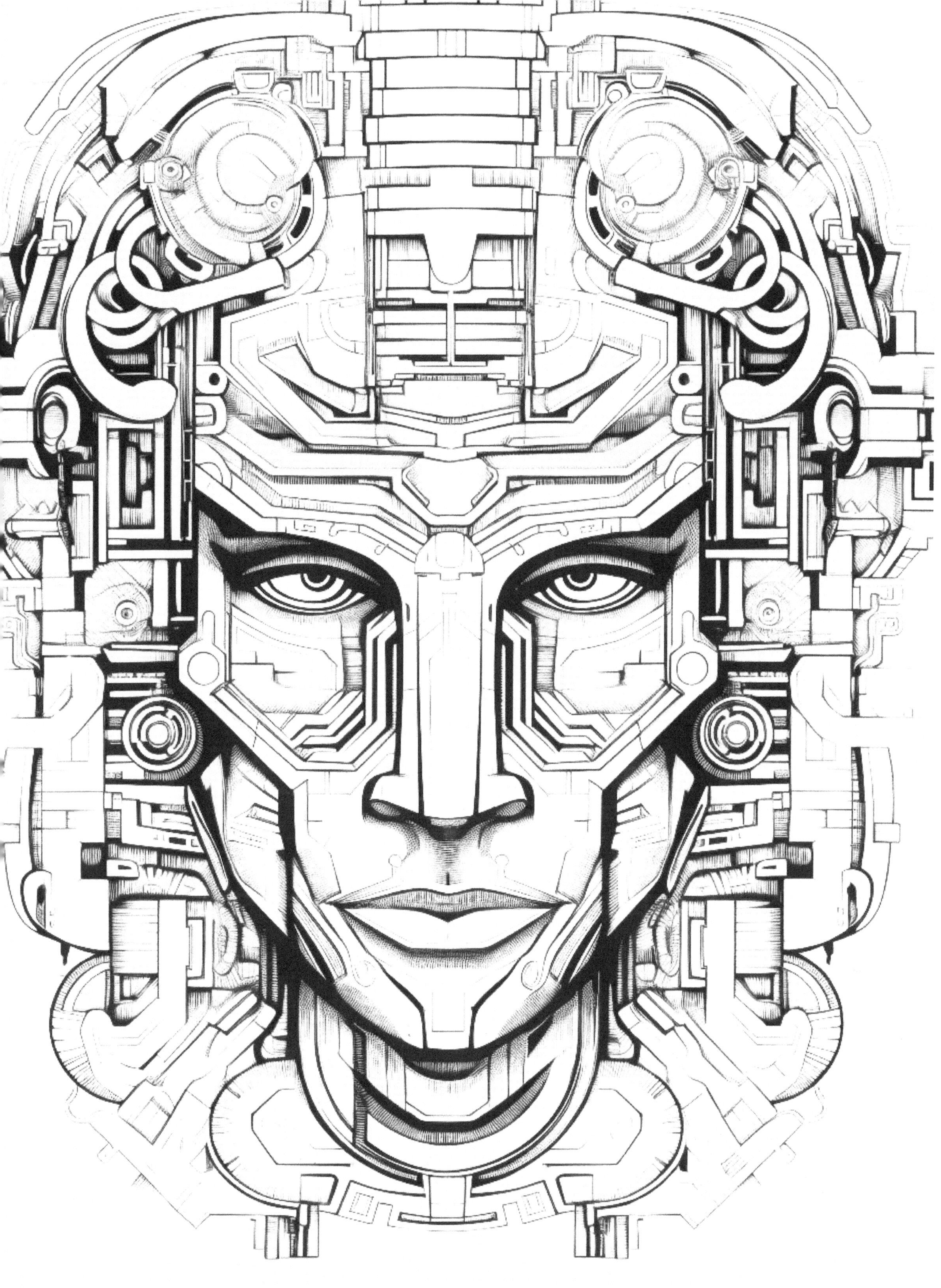

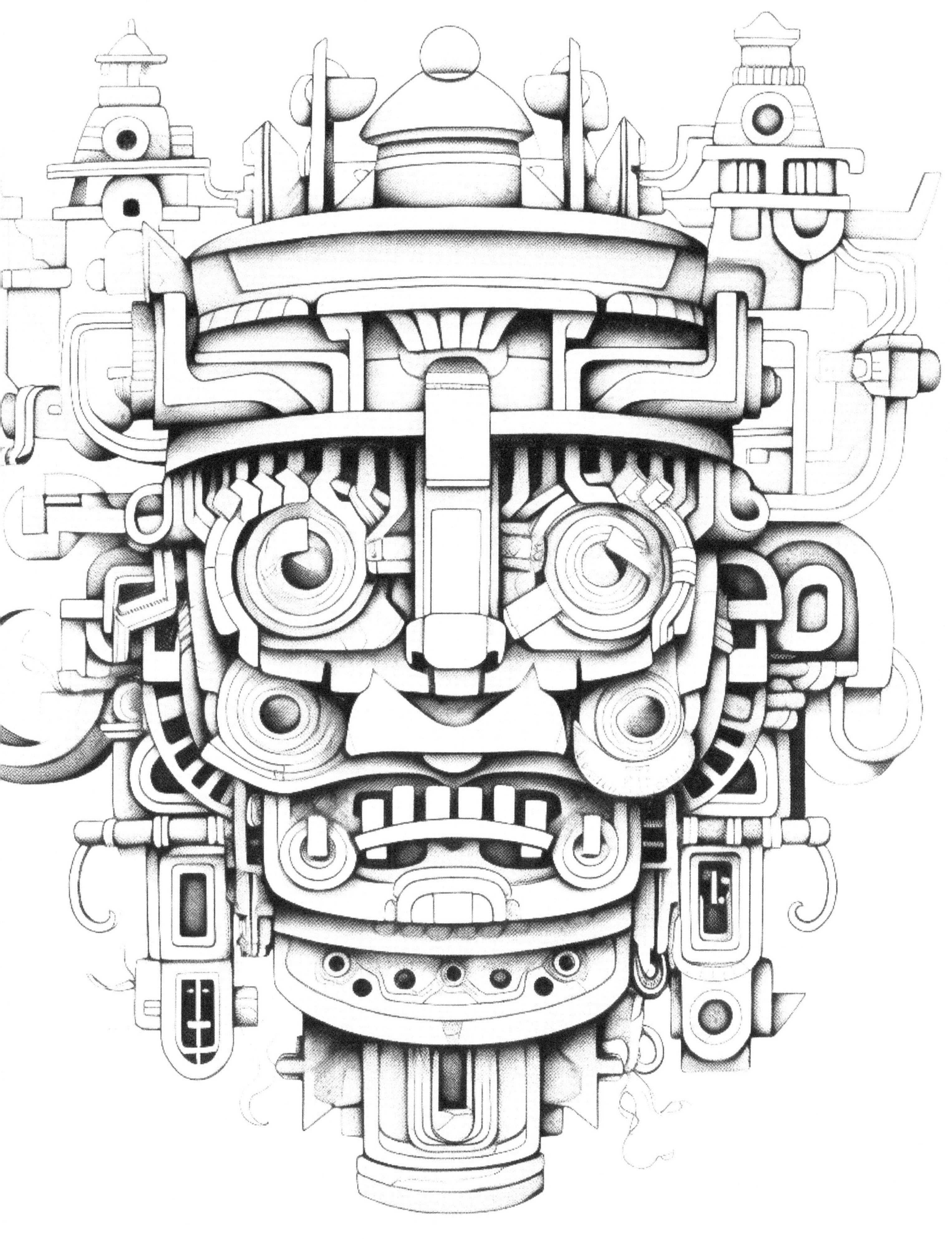

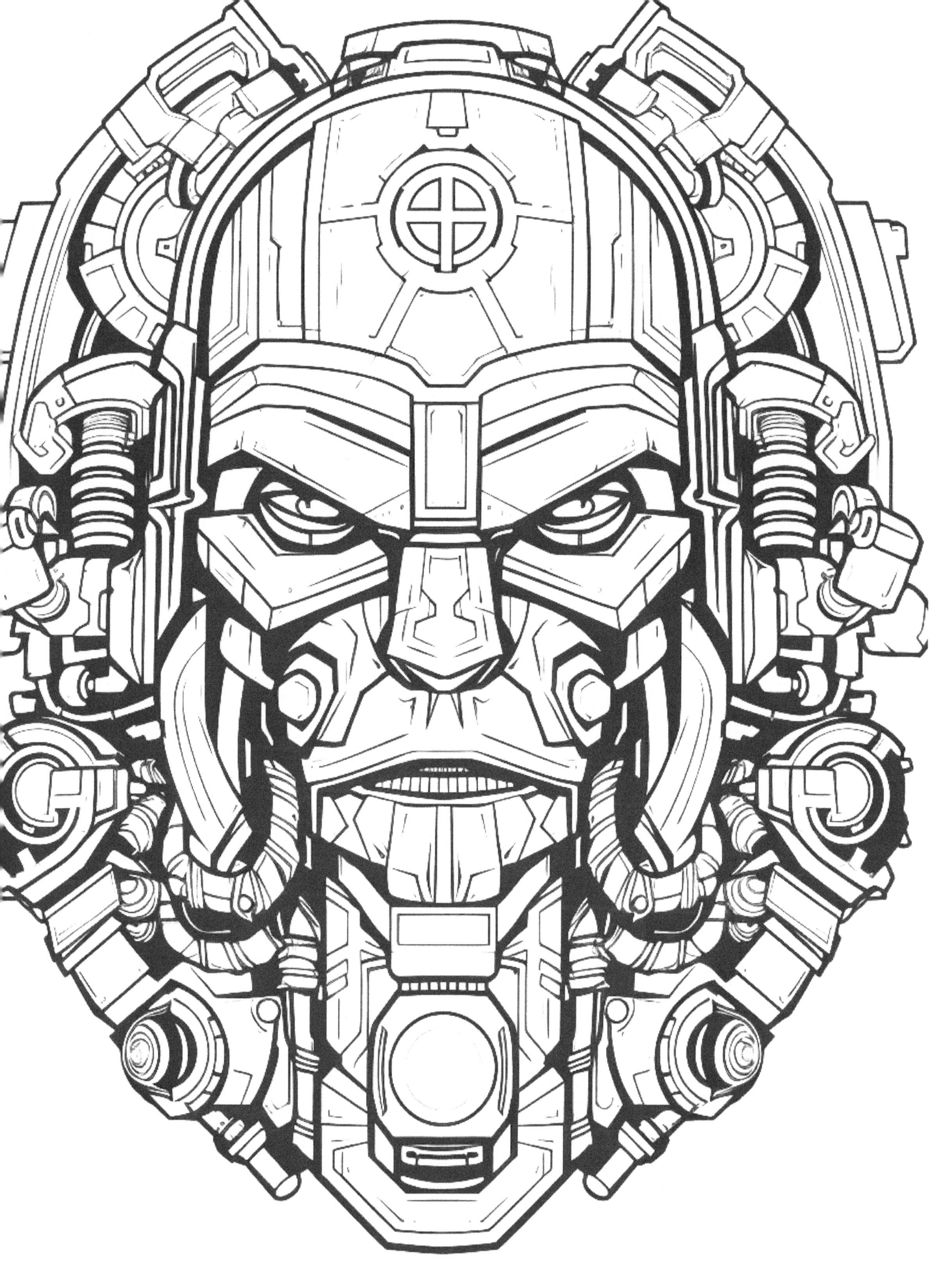

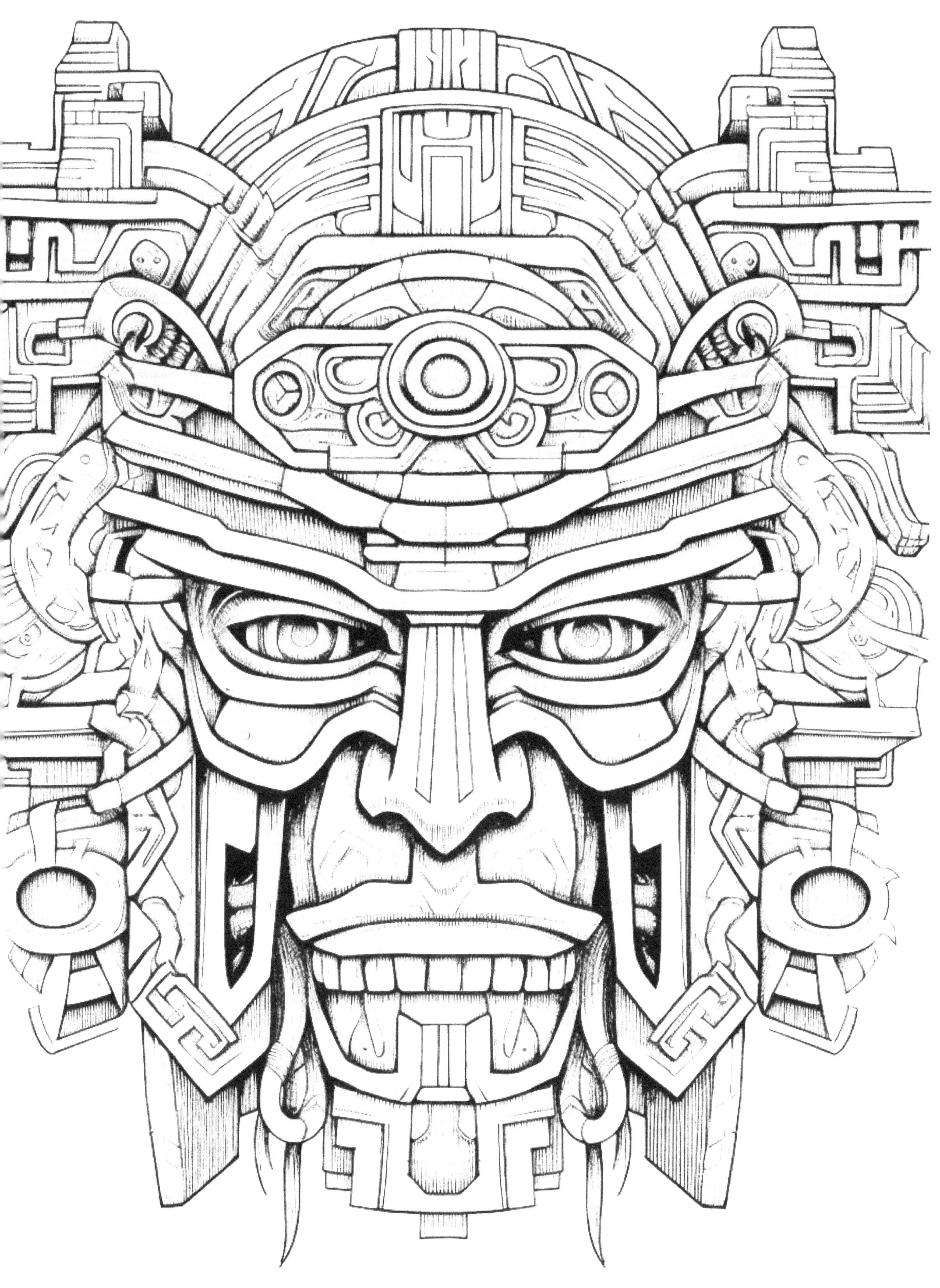

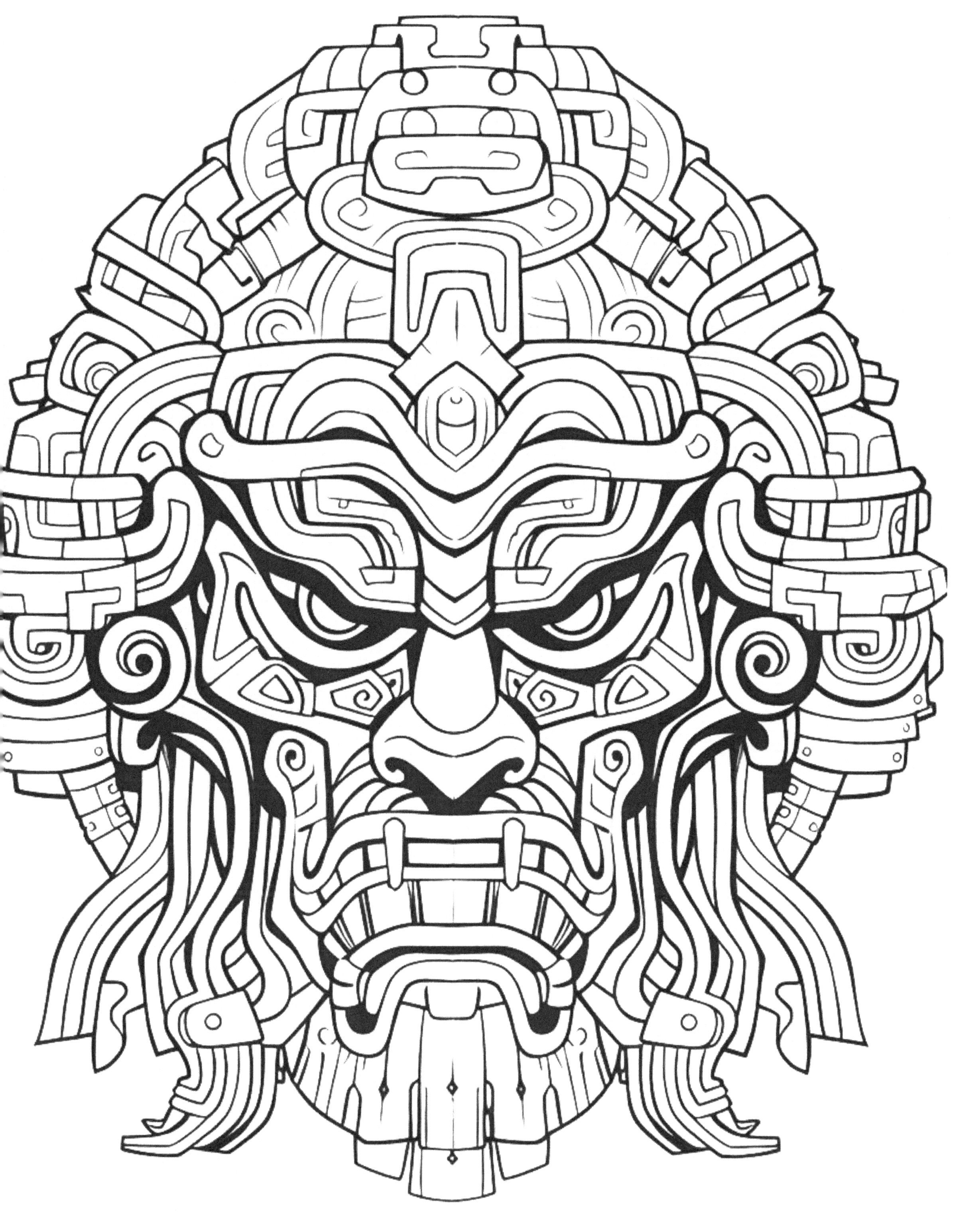

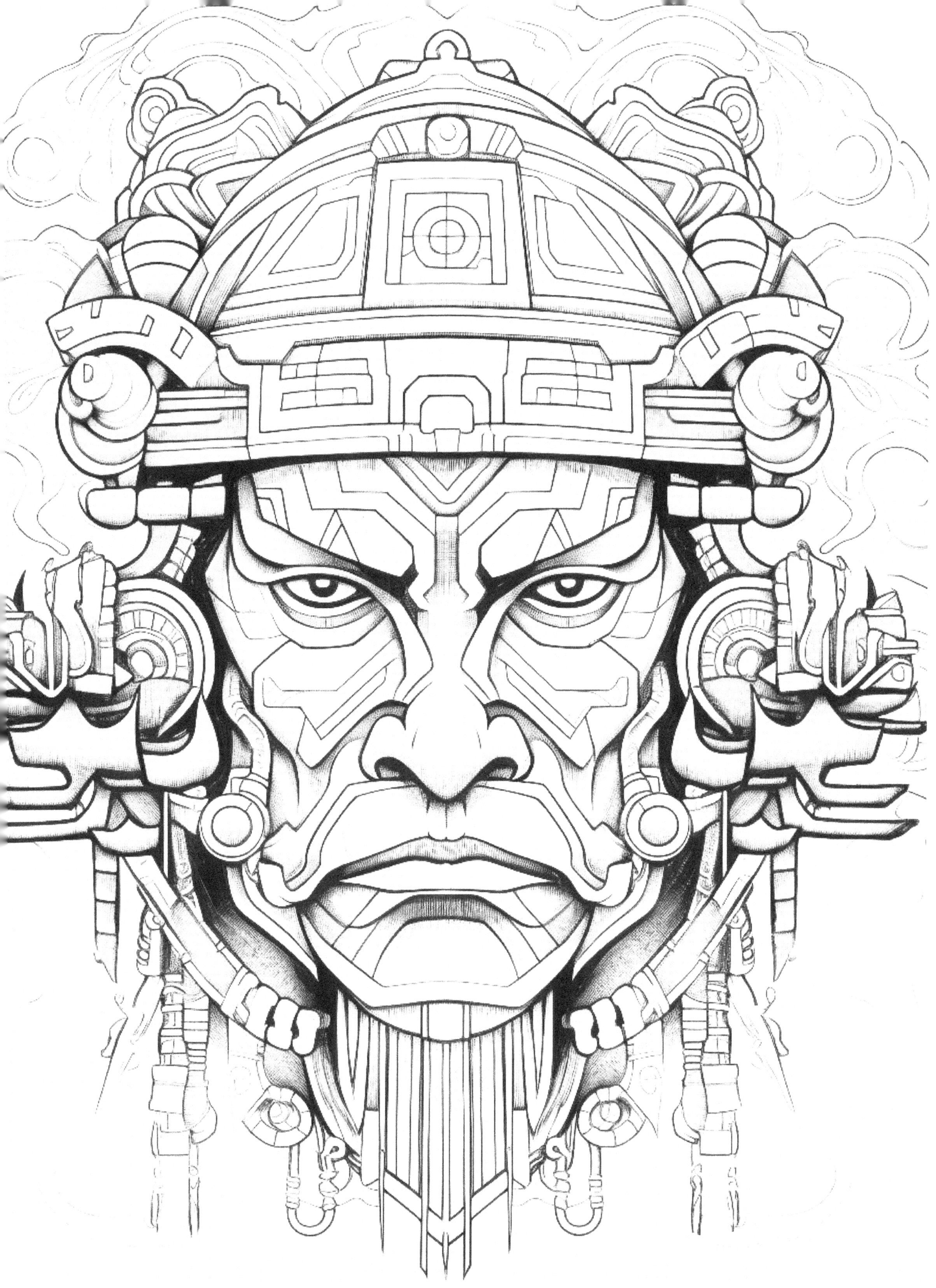

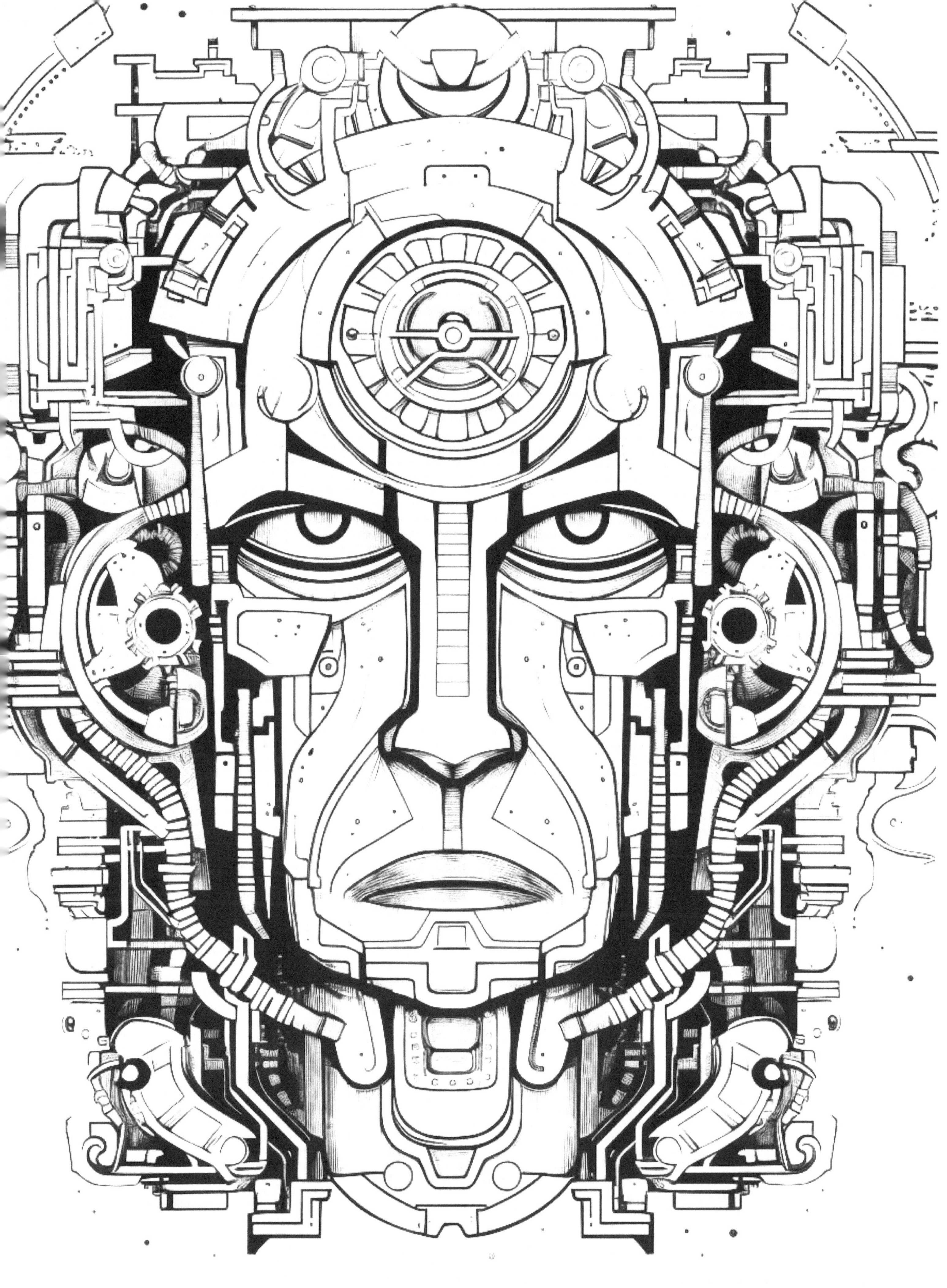

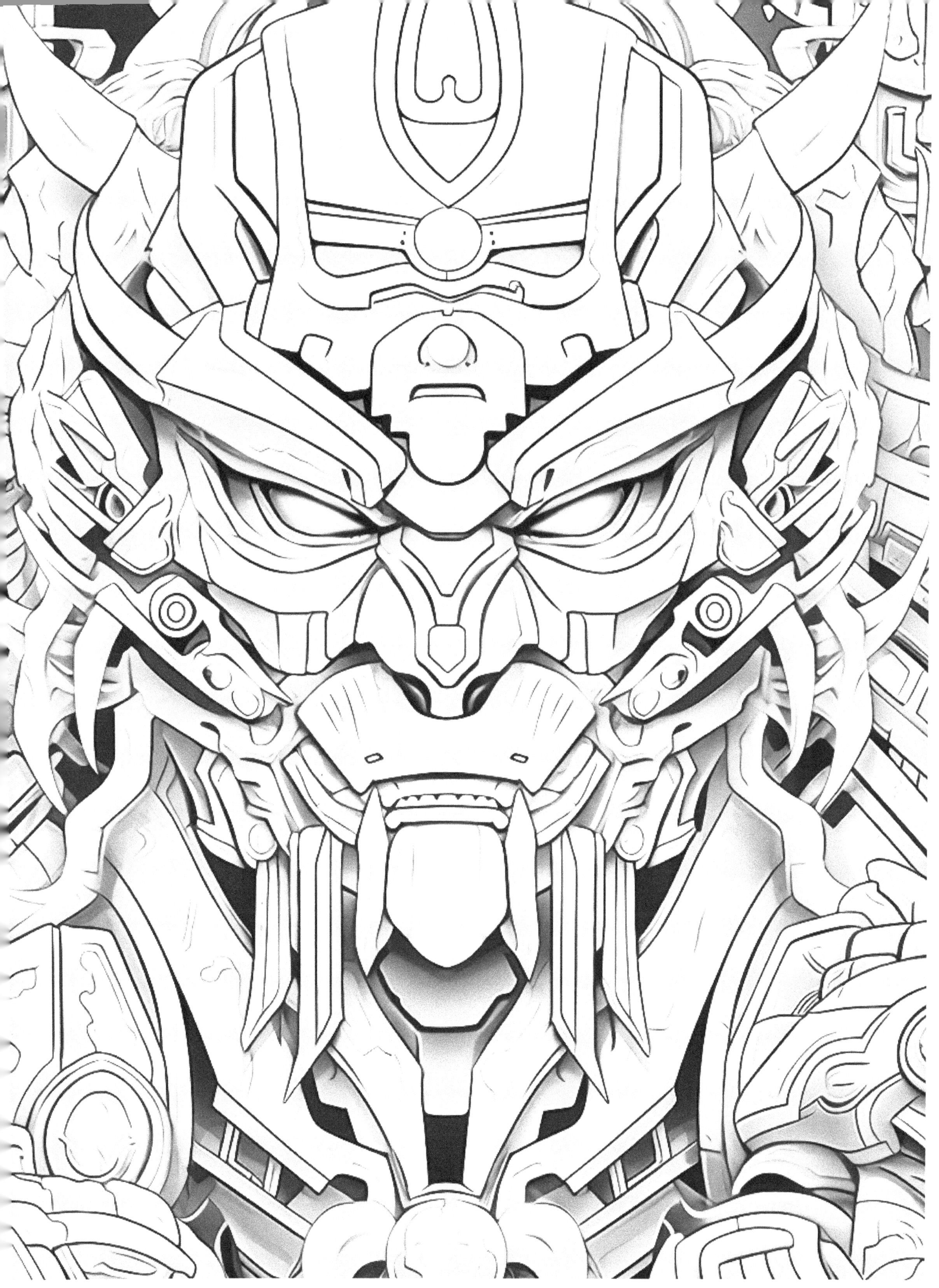